Praise for *Sh‹*

It has been said that God made people because God loves stories. In which case Irwin is one of God's most beloved. The stories in *Shechinah at the Art Institute* have many sources. Some are from the life experience of the author. Others have been passed from hand to hand for a thousand years. Still others are familiar as they are kin to the stories which shape our own lives. The wisdom, humor, and perspective in them all will enrich you and gently bind you to other lives both ancient and modern. A good story heals the loneliness which is the hidden wound of our time. Bravo Irwin. What a gift you have offered to us all.

—Rachel Naomi Remen MD, author of *Kitchen Table Wisdom* and *My Grandfather's Blessings*

I am not religious. But this book makes my heart sing. There's music in Irwin's words. Wisdom, too. He reminds me that in this darkened world, there is still light. And there is love. It's what makes this book not just entertaining, but important.

—Linda Ellerbee, journalist and author

Quirky, playful, steeped in classical Jewish learning, Keller unveils long-suppressed queerness in Jewish tradition and encounters the sacred miraculously appearing in the secular world.

—Rabbi Dr. Rachel Adler, author of *Engendering Judaism* and *Tales of the Holy Mysticat*

In these beautifully written meditations, Irwin Keller records his dialogue with sacred texts of his Jewish tradition. Ay, absolutely wonderful, so refreshing, hopeful in a world so desperate for peace.

—Greg Sarris, author of *Grand Avenue* and the forthcoming collection, *The Forgetters*

Irwin Keller, his ear trained on "the crosstalk of the Universe," knows when angels are about: in chance encounters, odd coincidences, dreams, and memories; even in the teeth of a vicious dog or the barrel of a gun. In Keller's luminous writings, these divine messengers reveal both the radiance within the everyday and the clouds that subdue the sacred. With this dazzling book, Keller takes his place among the messengers.

—Esther Schor, author of *Emma Lazarus*

A few pages into reading Reb Irwin Keller's luminous book, *Shechinah at the Art Institute*, I began mentally compiling a list of people I wanted to give a copy to. My father. My stepmother. My sister. My aunt. This friend who is Jewish. That one who is not. This is what Irwin does in his writings and in his life; he enlarges the circle, invites everyone in, mingling the secular with the spiritual with the skeptical with the bawdy with the beautiful. It's all there in this book, a record of a spiritual being having a very human experience and savoring the all in all of it. Pull up a chair, feast, enjoy.

—Alison Luterman, author of *In the Time of Great Fires* and *Desire Zoo*

In *Shechinah at the Art Institute*, the wondrous Rabbi Irwin Keller inhales all the world he inhabits and savors the details of all the miracles and realities of life. Rabbi Keller is one of the most kind, compassionate, brilliantly philosophical, thoughtful, and hilariously funny human beings. He understands that the past is always present. He understands that the past is part of us. This is something we should all understand.

—Lily Brett, author of *Too Many Men* and *Lola Bensky*

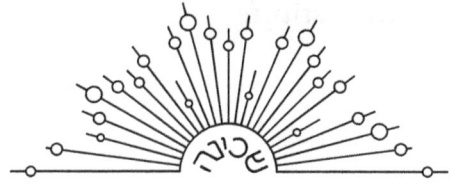

IRWIN KELLER

Shechinah
at the Art Institute

*Words * Worry * Wonder*

San Francisco | Fairfield | Delhi

Shechinah at the Art Institute
Irwin Keller

Copyright ©2024 by Irwin Keller

First Edition.

ISBN: 978-1-4218-3559-4

Library of Congress Cataloging-in-Publication Data

All rights reserved. Printed in the United States of America. No part of this book may be used or reproduced in any manner whatsoever without written permission except in the case of brief quotations embodied in critical articles and reviews.

Book design by Rodney Charles.
Cover design by Sasha O'Malley.
Cover painting by Mark Garrett.
Author photo by Adam Shemper.

An earlier version of "Postcards from the *Effeminati*" was published in *Liberating Gender for Jews and Allies: The Wisdom of Transkeit* (Cambridge Scholars' Press 2022). Earlier versions of "Shabbos-Fall in British Columbia" and "The Scent of Shechinah" were published in *In the Light of Peace* (Bayit Press 2021).

For information contact:

1ST WORLD LIBRARY
PO Box 2211
Fairfield, Iowa 52556
www.1stworldpublishing.com

BLUE LIGHT PRESS
www.bluelightpress.com
Email: bluelightpress@aol.com

Dedicated to the memory of my parents
Marilyn and Jerry Keller

Always with love.

Contents

Introduction . . .1
Shechinah at the Art Institute . . .3
Shabbos-Fall in British Columbia . . .8
When Max Janowski Sang Me to Sleep . . .10
Evening Prayer . . .15
At the Rebbe's Gay *Tish* . . .16
Double Solitaire . . .22
Bedside Pearls . . .27
Queer Medicine for Dark Times . . .32
How to Find God . . .36
The Theology of the Cubs . . .38
Angels and Airports . . .42
The Journey of Return . . .49
Postcards from the *Effeminati* . . .54
River of Light. . .61
City of Flowers and Stone . . .65
The Scent of Shechinah . . .70
Unlikely, Inevitable You . . .74
With Scott in the Crosswalk . . .78
Reflections of a Retiring Drag Queen . . .85
Minnie's Meringues . . .90
In Heaven's Court . . .95
The *Go'el* of *Boulevard de Sébastopol* . . .103

Reverse 23 . . .109
Ghost of *Shtetl* Future . . .110
Joseph's Bones . . .115
Such Stuff as Dreams are Made of . . .119
Oath of Disloyalty . . .124
The Parable of the Toyota in the Gully . . .126
The Bittersweet Exchange . . .132
Taking Sides . . .136
Glossary of Hebrew and Yiddish Terms . . .138
Acknowledgments . . .142
About the Author . . .144

"In the chequered area of human experience the seasons are all mingled as in the golden age: fruit and blossom hang together; in the same moment the sickle is reaping, and the seed is sprinkled; one tends the green cluster and another treads the wine-press. Nay, in each of our lives harvest and springtime are continually one, until Death himself gathers us and sows us anew in his invisible fields."

George Eliot, *Daniel Deronda*

Introduction

It's an odd and paradoxical thing living as a physical being. This incarnate life is frustratingly limiting. We are mired in the needs of our bodies, bound by gravity, trying to understand each other through the inefficiencies of language. We delight at music, beauty, flavor, and we are burdened with such terrible sorrow.

It's odd and paradoxical because even with – or maybe because of – the limitations of our bodies and lifespans, our species shares a powerful instinct that there is more than this incarnate life, that *we are more* than this incarnate life. This instinct persists and persists, despite the eyebrow-raising of our rational faculties.

I have been blessed to live a good incarnate life, in this body, on this Earth. I was born into a loving and funny family, and on that model co-created my own. As a child I heard a call to be a rabbi, or something like that. It was in part a longing to be a conduit of transmission, drawing the ancient into the future. And it was, on a body level, a call to explore the place where the incarnate and the transcendent touch.

In the early 1980s, I realized I couldn't be openly queer and get into any rabbinical school on the planet. I grieved that loss, which rolled right into the grief of the early AIDS epidemic. I cried, I protested, and I became a lawyer to try to be of service. I grieved and raged, but I also sang and mugged and provoked as Winnie of the Kinsey Sicks, America's Favorite Dragapella Beautyshop Quartet.

So much of that is behind me. The call to the rabbinate, banked like the coals of a campfire, blazed up in me again once there was oxygen to feed it. So now here I sit, a rabbi, flirting with ancient wisdom, the wisdom of my ancestors – the Jewish ones and the queer ones – who also looked for the place where the incarnate and the transcendent touch.

I breathe in, and the oxygen carries with it all of space and time, drawn into my lungs, which are themselves formed of impossibly old, repurposed earth and water, according to a DNA blueprint revised and re-revised by uncountable ancestors, their impulsive decisions and their deliberate decisions, their migrations, loves, hungers, and circumstances. I look at this world, past and future, with wonder. I look up at the stars full of curiosity. I am part of the Cosmos, of all that is seen and unseen. This body and this life are God's drag, the Infinite trying on a new way of being finite. I am grateful for all of it – all that has made it possible for me to taste this life when the odds are so against it. The improbability of my existence never escapes me.

Shechinah at the Art Institute

I ran into the Shechinah at the Art Institute of Chicago, the way it was when I was a kid. She was in one of the Impressionist rooms, in front of Seurat's *Sunday Afternoon on the Isle of la Grande Jatte*. It figured that she was in the Impressionist collection. She was standing there, multicolored like the paintings, drawing (and making) an impression.

She moved gently, gliding from canvas to canvas. She didn't read the descriptive text mounted on the walls. She knew the paintings and she knew the artists. She was, after all, their muse in a way. She was part of that Divine flow that pours into every blade of grass, every bird, lizard and rock, every haystack at sunset, and every painting of a haystack at sunset.

It was rare to see her so physical, emerging into three-dimensionality like the *impasto* of an oil painting. While she looked at the art, all eyes in the museum were on her. People who came that day had no idea why their attention was drawn off the images and onto this grand and near-solid figure, drifting from gallery to gallery. But they didn't feel like they missed out on seeing the paintings. They felt like they had seen all of them and more. They were filled with Cubism and portraiture and bronze Canaanite goddesses and the Jasper Johns alphabet painting that the Shechinah knows to be a sneaky kind of *gematria*.

I was feeling brave and a little infatuated, so I struck up a conversation. I asked her what brought her to the museum today. She reminded me about her grand tour. The tour she does every year, once a week, from Pesach through Shavuot, every seventh day of the *Omer*. Today was the day when, in kabbalistic cosmology, the quality of *Malchut* – the Immanent Divine and Sacred Feminine – would orbit through the house of *Tiferet*, the home of balance, truth, and beauty. And sure enough, here she was.

On the first week of the *Omer*, she told me, she had visited the realm of *Chesed* – kindness – stopping in on soup kitchens and classrooms, shadowing parents telling bedtime stories and urban gardeners with coffee cans of dirt and envelopes of seeds. In the second week, she was in the realm of *Gevurah*: the world of form and structure and limits, looking in on biologists, physicists, and engineers to see what they are learning and how they are responding to the unavoidable mechanics of the Universe.

"So this is art week?" I blurted out awkwardly. I felt my cheeks redden.

"This week is the realm of *Tiferet*," she said, "the world of beauty and balance. The marriage of form and feeling." As she said this, I realized we were in another gallery now, looking at water lilies, her own reflections somehow part of the reflection Monet painted onto the water. As we talked, we moved, floated almost, through the Art Institute without regard to stairs or walls or "Authorized Personnel Only" signs.

We found ourselves in the Thorne Rooms, an exhibit of 68 miniature interiors, like the most lavishly detailed dollhouses you could imagine, made by artist Narcissa Thorne in the 1930s and 40s, and donated to the museum in 1954, along with much of her fortune to pay for the upkeep of the tiny rooms. While critics argued about whether these tableaux were art, the public made the Thorne Rooms the Museum's most enduringly popular attraction.

I looked at the tiny interiors, the Shechinah at my side. I've loved these since I was young. I would nod approvingly at the medieval castles and renaissance villas, like everyone else, but my heart always leapt at the 1920s art deco interiors. They looked like tiny Fred Astaire movie sets: clean lines, rounded edges, gleaming polished floors just waiting for a tap dance, and windows looking out onto a starry urban night.

I used to come here as a child. Our great Aunt Anne – never married, world-traveled – would bring Lynn and me, and we would feel very grown up and fancy. We would look at the Thorne Rooms and a few pieces of art (Aunt Anne especially liked modern sculpture), and then we would sit in the café in the courtyard, at an umbrellaed table and have lunch together.

No sooner had this memory entered my head than the Shechinah and I were seated in the café in the great courtyard, the way it used to be. The Shechinah, now in bright sunlight, had for convenience's sake perhaps, taken the form of Aunt Anne, in a blouse with a Nehru collar, orange wooden beads, coral colored lipstick against her abidingly tan skin, and jet-black hair in a Vidal Sassoon cut. Sitting across from her, I was a child again, in a red blazer and clip-on tie. In front of me a grilled cheese sandwich off the children's menu waited, while the Shechinah poked at a scoop of tuna salad resting on a tomato splayed like a starfish.

I felt like I should keep up my end of the conversation so I asked her what she feels when she visits us in this way, and has it changed over the years. She said that she weeps for us, she weeps for our Exile. Not specifically our Jewish Exile, but our human Exile from the Divine. From the Divine in ourselves. From the Divine that pours through and is the stuff of this planet.

"But you know," she added, admiring a sprig of parsley on the side of her plate, "I have faith in you. I believe in you so much more than you believe in yourselves. You struggle and you hope, and you look at this moment in which you live, and you think all is lost. But I believe in you." She took a mouthful of tuna, chewed it thoughtfully and swallowed. "You see, it has to do with beauty. It's why we're here today."

"What does that mean?" I asked. "Just because humans can paint beautiful things?"

"No, no, it comes before painting beauty. It's *seeing* beauty. Why do you see beauty at all?" she asked.

I sat in silence. I'd never considered this. "I guess it's evolutionary," I said finally. "We see someone beautiful, we are attracted, and through this we propagate the species."

"Then why do you find a garden beautiful? Or a green landscape?"

"Maybe they suggest fertile places where we might be able to safely feed our tribe."

"Then why are cliffs beautiful? And deserts? And leopards and thunderstorms? These are dangerous things, but you see beauty in them too."

I ran out of comebacks and waited silently, hearing the nearby clatter of dishes and the distant roar of the elevated train. At last she continued.

"*Tiferet* is not beauty, but the quality in you that lets you see beauty. In attractive things and edible things and poisonous things too, in people and animals, and in moments that pierce your heart. *Tiferet* allows you to see the beauty in a painting of a water lily, even though it's not a water lily but crushed minerals mixed in oil."

"Okay," I stammered.

"I have faith in you because your ability to find beauty is returning. In time you – all of you – will come to find beauty in people who are not like you, in species that are not like you. You will find beauty in their longings, their sufferings, their deep hearts. You will appreciate that you are all painted – skillfully, I might add – with the same brush."

I heard her words but could only think about the divisions we make among ourselves, the abyss between humanity and all the rest of Creation, and I felt sad. She frowned, called a waiter over and ordered me a rainbow sherbet, even though I hadn't touched the grilled cheese.

"Listen," she said. "Don't give up hope. You are the Divine. You are like those Thorne Rooms. You are all miniatures, each of you capturing one face – no, one *interior* – of God. Not just humans. Everything is in the Divine image. Everything in this Creation is a miniature, made with such care and such detail. An experience of beauty or a beautiful experience – these are the moments when you notice it."

She took a breath and wiped the corners of her mouth with her napkin. She opened her glossy purse and reapplied her lipstick. "Listen kiddo, I do need to get going. There's something over at the Contemporary I want to catch. You okay?"

"Sure," I sputtered, rainbow sherbet cold and sticky in my mouth and iridescent on my spoon in the brilliant Chicago sun.

Shabbos-Fall in British Columbia

It's nearly Shabbos in British Columbia.

People sit in traffic on their way to dates and movies. They fiddle with the car radio and check the time on their cell phones.

Some have just gotten home, closing the door on a hard week. They drop bags and jackets and receive the embrace of well-worn armchairs.

Some Jews set tables and stir pots of soup like their great-grandmothers, except that jazz is playing, the soup has kale, and some of the stirrers are men.

In this pink twilight people hurry, turn on TVs, pour wine, open books. Dogs, elated, emerge into their evening walks, sniffing grass and trees and each other, tails curled in a question mark.

Even in the tall city sheathed in asphalt, the trees outnumber the people. The flowers outnumber the cars. The grass stretches from one end of the province to the other, Pacific to Rockies. Each blade of grass has a melody. If that melody had words, it might sound like *reach* or *dig* or simply, *I am. I am*, sings the grass.

A pair of angels – great, translucent, multicolored like rainbows on soap bubbles – survey the scene. They eye the whole province: seagulls shrieking over fishing boats, pencils working crossword puzzles, couples dozing on sofas, traffic roaring, Jews singing *Lecha Dodi*, rivers clapping over rocks, grass reaching, owls waking, all of life breathing.

The angels survey all of this, Shabbat falling in British Columbia.

One angel dissolves into a prayer which, if it were in words, would go: "So may it be again next week."

The other angel bursts into a scent of lilac, which, if it were in words, would go: "*Ken yehi ratzon*, may it be so."

And the grass responds, *I am.*

When Max Janowski Sang Me to Sleep

Every once in a while on Shabbat, I step outside of the guitar-and-drum expectations of my little Sonoma County shul, sit down at the piano, and sing the Chaim Nachman Bialik poem, *Shabbat Hamalkah – hachamah merosh ha'ilanot nistalkah*, "the sun is slipping behind the trees" – using, instead of its well-worn Israeli melody, a simple and stirring setting by Max Janowski.

Max Janowski was one of the great synagogue composers of the 20th Century. Prolific, although now known almost exclusively for his *Avinu Malkenu*, which was eventually yanked out of the synagogue and recorded by no less than Barbra Streisand herself, with a big, soupy orchestral arrangement and simplified chording by Marvin Hamlisch. I choose that setting of *Shabbat Hamalkah* for the same reason I watch developments like the Streisanding of *Avinu Malkenu* with interest. It is because I feel somewhat proprietary about Max Janowski's music. Because when I was little, Max Janowski used to sing me to sleep.

Well, not personally. And not every night. Just Tuesdays of summer.

It started when I was four or five. My parents had joined a brand-new congregation, called Beth Elohim, in Chicago's north suburbs. Although it wasn't the radical, artsy, mystical community that my Sonoma County synagogue is, it had a genuine freshness. Its families were all starting out with Baby Boom optimism, building tiny ranch houses on what had been Illinois prairie, amid budding schools and parks and shopping centers. The earth had been upturned and armored in a latticework of asphalt and cement. Saplings, held erect with tent ropes, bobbled on the newly laid lawns. The land seemed a blank slate, any memory of Potawatomi settlement reduced to myth or elementary school social studies projects. For these young urban expats, everything seemed possible. Including how to be Jewish.

In 1965, the families of Beth Elohim were offered the opportunity to merge with a much older synagogue, the seventy-plus-year-old B'nai Jehoshua, which resided in a magnificent but rapidly emptying building on Chicago's west side. B'nai Jehoshua's membership had been moving out to the suburbs, and the synagogue risked death by dispersal if it didn't establish an anchor further north. The merger happened, the beloved building was sold, and thus began the nomadic life of B'nai Jehoshua Beth Elohim.

Buildingless, we would welcome Shabbat at Niles Community Church, only blocks from my house. Oh, how I loved that church: the pews, the organ, the strangely non-Jewish orderliness! I loved sneaking away with my mother after the rabbi's sermon to set up the *Oneg Shabbat*. I was sometimes entrusted to make the punch — a block of ice, Hawaiian Punch, ginger ale, and rainbow sherbet, served up in soon-soggy Dixie Cups. Religious school took place at local public schools and the temple office was above a bowling alley. It sounds awkward and inconvenient, but it wasn't. It was thriving and exciting and new.

My father, Jerry Keller, was a popular bandleader in Chicago — a singer and sax man. The newly merged congregation might not have had much cash, but they knew their assets and sent emissaries to the house to recruit him to be BJBE's first choir director. Dad had never conducted a choir. What's more, he had grown up in a classical Reform synagogue where confirmation was offered instead of bar mitzvah, where Shabbat conveniently fell on Sunday, and where the officiant — back in Dad's day it was Felix Levy — was called minister. Dad's Jewish literacy was limited, despite being the great-grandson of a rabbi who had served at Berlin's monumental Neue Synagoge in the 1870s, during the residency of the great composer Louis Lewandowski as musical director – Lewandowski, whose *Lecha Dodi* and *Tzadik Katamar* are still on the menu at a wide range of synagogues, and whose *Kiddush* remains a staple 130 years later. But my father could read transliterated Hebrew as well as anyone. He was good with people and a fine musician, and he said yes.

That's when the choir moved into our house. A mismatched gaggle of 16 or so voices. They would ring the doorbell every Tuesday night of summer and spill into the house like the stateroom scene from *A Night at the Opera* in reverse. My mother would sing alto and set up the percolator. The men in the choir were largely amateurs, well-meaning non-musicians. But the sopranos, somehow, all had gorgeous voices. Big, vibrato-filled, operatic voices. I've sometimes wondered how that happened, how this confluence of gifted women ended up in the north suburbs, at the same moment, in the same synagogue. But the biggest voice of all belonged to our cantor, Harold Freeman. His Hebrew was often indistinct and his music reading sometimes impressionistic. But there was something deeply compelling — something of the Old-World *chazan* — in him, a cry in his voice that carried within it all the suffering and longing of Exile.

Every Tuesday night there they'd be, on the sofa and the folding chairs, gossiping more than singing, much to my father's frustration. Yet they loved him and eventually would sing beautifully, perhaps just to please him. And the repertoire? Well, the repertoire was almost entirely the work of Max Janowski.

Max was a Berliner as well, who emigrated to Japan and eventually Chicago on the eve of the War. He was a formidable musician (eventually writing over 500 pieces of music) and a larger-than-life personality. I can't quite explain his widespread popularity in American Reform synagogues; I'll let the musicologists figure out his place in the canon. His pieces were often difficult — hard to sing, sometimes overwhelming to listen to, and I understand he took a certain pride in that. But, especially when simpler, his music was stunningly beautiful. As an heir to the German Jewish composers, he had no allergy to choirs and pipe organs. He came from the same tradition as fellow Berliner Louis Lewandowski and Austrian composer Salomon Sulzer, whose choir and pipe-organ setting of the *Shema* is now so universal that people imagine it to be ancient and Orthodox. But Max's compositions had — dare I say it? — a less churchy ring. They weren't about the glorious space of the cathedral or even the great synagogue; they came from somewhere internal, the product of the deep and abiding sorrow and bitterness and yearning of the Jews. Even his gentlest and most intimate pieces, like *Shabbat Hamalkah*, feel like a stolen moment of sweetness in a hostile world.

In 2012, it was Max's centennial, and I attended some concerts memorializing him. When I was a teenager, I sang in a choir under his baton; later I taught Hebrew school at the South Side synagogue where he was the musical director. I realize now he was barely in his 60s when I knew him, but to me, with his thinning hair, buttoned-up manner, and German accent, he already seemed 100.

Our next cantor at BJBE was a whippersnapper. Just 10 years older than I was, Cory Winter was himself a Max Janowski protégé. He had sung for Max since he was a boy soprano, and Max treated him as a musical heir. Later, Cory would become my own friend and mentor, which, I sometimes like to think makes Max Janowski my grandmentor.

Tuesday nights as a child, the choir would sit in our living room with their sheet music and their coffee, and they would sing.

I would get sent to bed, where I would fall asleep to the lullaby of their chatter, their dirty jokes, and Max Janowski's triumphant and tearjerking chords. These would seep into my slumber and my cells, these chords, both modern and ancient, deep and soaring, heartening and heartrending. They would enter my body like a transfusion. By the time High Holy Days arrived, I would sit with the adults and not with the other kids, expectant, waiting for the choir to stand and sing not Max Janowski's music, but mine.

On the *bimah*, as in my Tuesday night dreams, they would petition God to be heard. *Shema Koleynu*, they would sing – "Hear our voice!" – as the chord progression ached with pathos under a carefully maintained surface of calm. They would call out for peace – *Sim Shalom* – solemnly, resolutely, as if to give the Divine one more chance.

And amid all this grandeur, they would humble themselves – *Avinu Malkenu*, we have gone astray but hear us anyway! — with chording that was both rich and lonely. Every human in that sanctuary would try to fight back tears and fail.

High Holy Days were the yearly triumph of this music, ringing out, belonging to the full congregation and to God. But on the Tuesday nights of my childhood, those summer Tuesday nights, Max's melodies would enfold me like a blanket. They would make my house Jewish and make the world Jewish. They would seep out of the double-paned windows and dance under the suburban stars, treading lightly on the new sod where the crickets had only just begun to sing.

Evening Prayer

Blessed are You, Great Mother.
You summon the evening.
And in the deepening darkness,
You open the shutters and change out the seasons,
folding winter into the cedar chest,
shaking mothballs out of seersucker spring.
You set stars spinning in orbits –
a fancy juggler, plates on poles.
You work the wheel of time,
darkness from light and light from darkness,
filaments of day, night, day, night.
Blessed are You, Great Mother,
Weaver of Evening.

At the Rebbe's Gay *Tish*

If this were a Chasidic tale, it might begin with a journey. Maybe a famous rabbi in disguise as a pauper, visiting poor households and offering miraculous blessings. Or perhaps someone traveling to a great city to arrange a marriage or find a cure or sell an old wagon. On the journey there might be an unexpected obstacle – a horse goes lame, a river floods, or Shabbos falls early.

It was August, and I was beginning a journey from Manhattan, where I had overnighted, to the foothills of the Berkshires for Camp Nehirim, a sorta-real, sorta-ironic summer camp experience for gay Jewish men. My accidental seatmate on the train was an Orthodox Jewish guy, with a tractate of Talmud on his tray table. I asked what he was studying.

"Talmud," he answered.

"I know, but which volume?"

After registering surprise that I knew enough to ask that question, his eyes darted around nervously. "*Niddah*," he whispered. *Niddah* is the tractate about women's purity and menstruation. His face reddened. "I never had the chance to study it when I was young," he added, looking like he'd been caught with his hands in his mother's dresser drawers.

If this were a Chasidic tale, the unexpected traveling companion would maybe be a supernatural figure, posing as flesh and blood. Maybe an angel, maybe a demon. And when I get caught up in conversation with someone who is Orthodox, I am open to the angel, but I confess that I tend to expect the demon. I expect that as he gets to know me, I will be judged and condemned, the naked-headed gay guy who talks Torah but drives on Shabbos. I would be the demon in his tale.

But I was feeling happy that morning, elevated. I had invoked angels to accompany me on this journey, the first time I'd ever explicitly done so, so my outlook was expansive and other-worldly. I took the risk of conversation, and soon we were, to my surprise, studying together – not *Niddah*, which stayed resolutely shut, but a project of mine. An hour in, he asked me where I was heading. "To a gay Jewish retreat," I answered.

Ba-bum. Ba-bum. Ba-bum. Our hearts marked time while our eyes remained riveted to the back of the seats in front of us, the Hudson Valley flying past the window.

"So, you're gay?" he asked.

"Yes I am."

I braced myself for an as-yet unformulated unpleasantness. Instead, he dropped his head, sighed, and said, "It's terrible what happened in Jerusalem last week." Meaning the murder of a 16-year-old girl by a crazed Orthodox man at the Jerusalem Pride Parade. I was caught off guard by his compassion and his sad tone, as if he were apologizing for both the incident and his own helplessness. My surprise was not unlike the surprise of so many Chasidim in so many stories, when the rebbe reveals unexpected magical knowledge of a joy or a tragedy that his disciples had not perceived.

"Yes, terrible," I replied. We sat in silence for some minutes, and then resumed our study.

Eventually I arrived at Easton Mountain Retreat Center in Greenwich ("Green-Witch" not "Grennitch"), New York. And green Greenwich certainly was. Coming from thirsty California, the expanses of soft grass and the array of ponds and lakes seemed immodest almost to the point of vulgarity.

Once there I met the week's other faculty members, people who, until I knew them better, I understood simply as the rabbi, the cantor, the yoga guy, the nature guy, and the porn actor. We reviewed the schedule and got to work. My docket included teaching a class every day of the retreat, leading the Friday night service, and presiding over a late night *tish*, modeled on a Rebbe's *tish* of old, where I would tell stories and lead us in *niggunim*.

The participants began to roll in, the way Chasidim would pour into Bratzlav or Berditchev or Lublin, to spend the Jewish holiday at the *shtibl* and table of their favorite rebbe. Instead of Yisroels and Motls and Shmuels, we had Steves and Marks and Sams – several of each, in fact. Instead of gabardines and *shtreimlech*, we had shorts, tank tops, and by the pool and in the pond we used as a *mikveh*, nothing at all.

These were guys of a certain age who had all experienced struggle. They had faced homophobia, they had lost lovers and friends to AIDS, and they had faced exclusion in the Jewish world because they were gay. So here they were to do some reclaiming of Jewish turf together. Some of them were living very active Jewish lives; some were returning to Judaism after long absences. Many had been instrumental in forming gay synagogues on the east coast, where they defiantly re-created the more conservative observance of their childhoods. I was struck at how, in a group of 50 Jewish gay men, I still felt at the fringe in terms of my own Jewish practice. However, I was pleased to discover I was not the only one there who welcomed Shabbos in a skirt.

I led Kabbalat Shabbat with the cantor. As soon as I began speaking, I became aware that how I do it, commonplace in my home community, was completely new for most of them. I could see their surprise at the visualizations and the punch lines, the sexy talk, and the use of Cole Porter's "Night and Day" as our *ma'ariv aravim* prayer. I readied myself for resistance, but they gave themselves over to the music and the newness, and the night got higher and higher.

We kept getting higher and higher. After Shabbos dinner we settled in for the *tish*. For an hour or more, in a small room of dinner tables and folding chairs, we sang *niggunim* – wordless melodies – and I told stories, two from the Chasidic world and one from the trusty Sages of Chelm repertoire. One of the two Chasidic stories was about women. There are not as many of those stories as there are about the Chasidic Rebbes, but they do exist. They are usually about *rebbetzins*, wives of well-known Rebbes. Such *rebbetzin* stories typically tell of her generosity or her cooking, both of which are taken in this literature as expressions of piety and nearness to God, and are set out as an example for women and men alike. Beautiful, sweet, non-revolutionary stories. I brought the *rebbetzin* story because in this male-only space, in this somewhat but not completely tongue-in-cheek re-enactment of a Chasidic court, I was beginning to feel uncomfortable in my chair and in my body.

I confess I love the ecstatic singing and storytelling of the Chasidim, ever since a weekend in high school that I spent at the Lubavitch House in Milwaukee. As a man (for most intents and purposes), loving that stuff is a privilege I have access to. But in my non-nostalgic waking life, it's not so easy. I am not able or willing to pray or celebrate somewhere in which women are barred from leadership and kept out of the room; or where women's public voices are considered *treyf*; or where my own family and hard-earned life would be considered *treyf* if anyone bothered to ask about it.

So I no longer pray with Chabad, no matter how good a party they throw, no matter how sweet the singing, no matter how much I need to say *kaddish*. Caught between these truths, that sometimes men-only space is for healing and sometimes men-only space is a gleeful display of patriarchy, there we were. A room full of men, just men, singing.

And the singing was celestial because these were not just random men. These were four dozen gay Jewish men. "Artsy" men, as our great aunts referred to us euphemistically. Some of them were fine professional musicians; some were vocally trained. I'd guess 80% of them had been in all their high school musicals, and a good number of those kept up their chops at piano bars up and down the eastern seaboard. These guys could sing, and they could harmonize. The walls of the room trembled with the splendor of it. They were a heavenly choir of first and second tenors, baritones and basses. Melodies poured out and fists on tables kept time. I couldn't help but have the overwhelming sense that we were some European *yeshivah*, or some lively rabbinic court, the way they are described in the Chasidic stories.

If this were a Chasidic story, there would now be a twist. The triumph of an underdog. God accepting the prayer of an outcast over the objection of the rebbe's disciples. Or maybe the Prophet Elijah would be revealed at a key moment in the form of a beggar at the door, and the behavior of all the players would be evaluated in a different light. I awaited the twist.

We sat and sang and the room rocked. It felt impossible that fewer than 50 men could make music this big. I suddenly had a vision of other souls emerging into the room. *Yeshivah bochers* of centuries past. The ones who spent their youths in love with their study partners and for whom the subtext of love was supplanted by the text of Talmud. The ones for whom desire was requited only by debate. The ones for whom there was no path of fulfillment that included both spirit and body, and who did the best they could to play the roles expected of them, riddled though they might have been by guilt and despair. The ones for whom, perhaps, it was enough back then, but for whom today, it would not be.

I felt these souls fluttering into the room to join us, a trace of worn leather tefillin and musty books in the air. I felt them taking their places on the few empty folding chairs, or sitting on tables, or leaning on shoulders, or perching in the rafters. I imagined I heard their voices singing out as loudly as we were singing. And we, who had struggled to reclaim a piece of Judaism for ourselves, managed to create for a moment a safe place for them.

I'm not sure anyone saw this other than me, although it might be that everyone did. But in that moment, the voices of the yoga guy and the porn guy and the nature guy, the voices of men in pastel polos and men in white Shabbos shirts and men in skirts rose up, with the counterpoint of skilled musicians and a cry of deep longing, eventually causing the roof itself to crack right open, carrying an unspoken prayer for a more loving world. The music of all these men flew up, like a pillar of flame, straight to heaven.

Double Solitaire

It's the most wonderful time of the year.

I was looking forward to a most wonderful interfaith Solstice Shabbat that our Sonoma County congregation hosts each December. We sit in a circle, tea lights everywhere, offering Hebrew chants, chants of the ecumenical Christian Taizé community of France, words from the Quran, and teachings about the nurturing dark and the returning light. The chanting would be led by my friend Atzilah, and in the chill air this community of spirited people from a range of religious backgrounds and practices would come together and share elements of religion's deep structure: the telling of time and passage of days, the waning and waxing of the sun, and the renewal of the Divine that seems to be born in these winter days.

I was looking forward to all of this, but America was on the move that day and my mother and I, like thousands of others, found ourselves stranded in snow at O'Hare Airport in Chicago, our flight cancelled, and our hope of attending the Winter Treasures service rapidly fading. Amidst the crowds, it seemed the entire US military was on holiday furlough. In fact, they were all sitting in the food court in uniform, eating their Panda Express rations as they headed home to families across the country.

A young man sat next to us at a large communal table. I say "man," but had he not been in Navy uniform, I'd have guessed him to be a boy of 16. He seemed curious about us and struck up small talk with my mother, who as is well known, was a small-talk magnet in public places. He was stationed in Hawaii and was on a layover heading to his parents in Connecticut. New Haven. Christmas. "Do you celebrate Christmas?" he asked us.

"No, we're Jewish," I said. "Our winter holiday came early this year, so we're just looking forward to the quiet time."

"Ah," he said, momentarily at a loss. "When I was little, I didn't care about Christmas either. Just about the presents. But then I began appreciating Jesus and would say, 'Thank you Jesus for being born.' Now I've let Jesus into my life."

"Ah," I said, my mind already racing with how to respond to where this seemed to be going.

"I hope you'll think about letting Jesus into your life," he concluded.

"Well," I said, not wanting to completely dash his hopes for our salvation, "we'll give it thought. Thanks." My mother and I began dealing out two decks of cards in hopes that a game of double solitaire would neatly sew up the situation. But he continued to chat.

"So, where do you live? Where are you going?" he asked.

"My mother lives here in Chicago. I live in California with my husband and co-parents and children, and Mom is coming to visit." I offered this information thinking, naively, that a quick revelation of same-sex marriage and alternative family might put an end to the campaign for our souls. Maybe the blessing of homosexuality would serve, where double solitaire was failing, to put an end to this moment of increasingly awkward interfaith relations.

No such luck. Our sailor continued, "Well, I hope you'll read some of what Jesus wrote and let him into your life." He looked at me eagerly, on the edge of his seat, waiting for my moment of revelation and redemption.

I was dealing out the next hand now, the blood of generations of persecuted ancestors pumping vigorously through my veins. I entertained the possibility that this stranger was Elijah, the prophet, showing up as always in disguise to test our compassion. Then I reasoned that Elijah probably wouldn't require me to go as far as accepting Jesus as my personal savior as an act of kindness to satisfy a stranger. So, I made the decision – perhaps not the best one – to address this head on.

"Listen," I said, "I appreciate how much finding Jesus has meant to you. I think Jesus had some fantastic and radical things to say, but I don't believe him to be God or the son of God or in charge of my soul. And," I continued, now on a roll, "it's not polite to push your religious beliefs on others."

This last add-on was admittedly disingenuous. Disingenous because discussing religion is not inherently impolite. Or shouldn't be. It is only impolite because we've not done well at having those conversations in America or maybe anywhere, and we get possessive and upset. In the best of all worlds, we could share freely about our spiritual yearnings and practices; we could hear each other's experiences with curiosity and excitement. But in practice, it often feels like a turf war, and in some religions' doctrines, it explicitly is. I had felt my anger and defensiveness welling up, and a lesson on courtesy seemed the quickest, if most superficial, way to end the skirmish.

"I'm not trying to force it on you," he said at last. "I was just offering it as a suggestion."

Our friend pouted, worrying he'd offended us. I felt like I'd kicked a puppy. Plus, he was a sailor on active duty, and I had violated our nation's strict code of deference and decorum toward service members. I tried to defuse his anxiety and my own prickliness by changing topics and explaining to him how to play double solitaire, all the time worrying that he would now think Jews care more about playing cards than about either salvation or the national defense.

I began dealing my hand. "There are mixed goals," I told him.

"You want to play more cards than anyone else. But you can only do that if everyone has a good game. It's both competitive and collaborative, and you must hold both of those intentions as you play. That's what makes it sometimes confusing and that's what makes it fun."

As I said this, the game offered itself up as a model for how we might all live together in this diverse world. You must be committed to your own hand; you must have hope for your own success; that is natural. But the game is more satisfying for you – and everyone – when you accept the integrity of other players' hands, and root – even just a little bit – for their success as well. My own game was often improved by my mother, a superior player, looking up from her hand and theatrically clearing her throat to draw my attention to an important card I had left unplayed.

With double (or triple or quadruple) solitaire, the play is more fun than the win. In a better world it might be that way for the interplay of our religions and backgrounds – the cards we were dealt. As the Jewish visionary Mordecai says in George Eliot's 1876 novel, *Daniel Deronda*, "[It] is a vain question . . . whether our people would beat the rest of the world. Each nation has its own work, and is a member of the world, enriched by the work of each." My own teacher, Rabbi Zalman Schachter Shalomi, visualized the world as a body, each *ethnos* an organ carrying out its own indispensable function. All the organs must be nourished for the sake of the whole; there is no question of any individual organ *winning*. I turned to my cards and began looking for my next move.

Hours later, it was time to board. The sun was down, and we had missed the Winter Treasures Shabbat service. The terminal was still packed, babies crying, people spilling salads and talking on cell phones. A great cacophony of voices and experiences and outlooks. This is a crowded world, so crowded, and everyone is just trying to get home.

Right where I was, I closed my eyes to welcome Shabbat, which shows up even in crowded airports – Shabbat which is, to my mind, the most wonderful time of the year. But I'm biased.

Bedside Pearls

It was late fall, and a dozen days since my mother, visiting from Chicago, had a stroke while sitting next to me in the car. Heading to lunch, we changed our destination to the emergency room, a sluggish, high-speed drive, during which Mom, becoming aware of how badly this might go, looked at me and said, "Shit. Shit."

It had been a good day. She'd arrived the night before and we'd gone to a concert. In the morning I gave her homemade borscht and sour cream, one of her favorite treats. Then we'd gone to my Yiddish poetry class, where I taught a poem by Kadya Molodovsky, in which she asks God to help her give up this painful world and to send His most beautiful angel for her so that her last gaze might be extinguished with a smile.

Once installed in the ICU, Mom sank into and tentatively returned from unconsciousness. Then the community arrived. Our friend Shari dispensed with her week's plans in order to coordinate for us. Relatives from back home, as well as friends from Mom's synagogue and her PFLAG community, began calling and texting.

In Torah that week, Joseph was sitting vigil at his father's bedside – his 147-year-old father, from whom he had long been separated, but who, unforeseen, or perhaps completely foreseen by Joseph, the interpreter of dreams, had ended up coming to him in Egypt and was now literally embedded in a place where Joseph could keep company and give care. Like Joseph, I ended up far away from my birthplace. Like Joseph, I'd lived with constant anxiety about a distant parent. And like Joseph, I found, beyond all reasonable expectation, a parent on my own doorstep in a moment of great need. I imagine that Joseph's mind wandered to the question of *bashertness*, however that was said in ancient Egyptian.

Joseph seemed to think it was all meant to be: Pharaoh's dreams, the rationing plan, the famine itself. So that Jacob would end up not in Hebron, near the graves of Isaac and Rebecca, but in Egypt, on Joseph's turf, where Joseph could rally the best healers and magicians and musicians. So that Jacob could be comfortable in his last days, in a safe and cozy bed, with his children and grandchildren in attendance.

We were similarly fortunate. For decades I lived with the dread: what if Mom's life-changing event (because we will all have one, whether disease or disaster or death) happens while she's alone in her house? This sudden stroke resolved my decades-old anxiety. The cards were dealt, and my mother ended up close by, in my car, and for a short number of weeks, in a hospital just a few miles from my house. We were able to marshal remarkable resources for her – healers, magicians, musicians. Including my sister, who walked away from a Broadway tour so she could simply be there.

We had some magnificent moments in the hospital room. An Erev Shabbat in the ICU more intense and magical than any I could hope to achieve on the *bimah*, with contraband Manischewitz smuggled in by one of the doctors. And, briefly, moments of recovery. The first half-smile. An attempt to form a word. The squeeze of a hand. A reaction to a song or story or voice or face. A soft moaning that shifted in pitch until it matched a *niggun* being sung around the bedside. Each of these was a treasure. I felt like a diver discovering an oyster bed and finding pearl after pearl. Not in every oyster, but enough to make me not give up the dive.

Joseph must have felt such extraordinary mindfulness at his father's bedside. Torah tells of him prostrating himself, but in my mind's eye I see him not bowing but collapsing from grief. He'd been without his father for so many years; now he was to lose him a second time. I wonder if Joseph told his father the old stories. I wonder if he said, "I love you." Their relationship was complicated; what healing happened at the end?

With my mother, there was nothing left unsaid. She was an insistent articulator of love, through her words and her actions. She loved freely and extravagantly, taking people under her wing with ease. I told a young ICU nurse, "If my mother were awake, she would ask you how you came to be a nurse and tell you how proud your parents must be." Speaking words of love and encouragement was simply her way. Nothing left unsaid, no endearments missing.

Time slowed down during those weeks, and I noticed every precious moment. But I was also misled by my heightened, adrenaline-infused mindfulness, lulled by the strength and beauty of the support we were offered. I felt proudly in control of a difficult situation. Friends back in Chicago were checking on the house; mail was being forwarded; doctors were consulted. A Facebook group was announcing updates on Mom's condition to well over 200 loved ones and admirers, like a town crier, or like the beadle in the Chelm story, who would rap on everyone's shutters to announce the coming of Shabbos, until he was too old and frail to do the walk. So everyone in the town agreed to unhinge their shutters and bring them to the synagogue so he could rap on them all in one place.

I felt so in charge of things that, determined to demonstrate the self-care people encouraged me to exercise, I scheduled a haircut, followed by a bodywork session to take care of my back, which had been in spasm for weeks before the stroke. I was proud to be taking care of myself. Glad that Mom was safe at the hospital with my sister. The terrific nurses had their eyes on her. Congregants and friends were on the case: Shoshana was coming to give her reiki; Atzilah would be coming to chant; Mac was heading over to read her children's stories from Kipling. Yes, all things considered, this was going okay, and I was feeling very in charge of an otherwise dire situation.

But I learned that I was not in charge of it all. You cannot be in charge of it all. This was explained to me not in words, and not by any person but by the Universe, in the form of a large dog, a Catahoula Hound that I walked past on the way from my haircut, a creature that was perhaps frustrated with the terms under which it was living its life. This unfamiliar familiar conveyed to me the message that we cannot count on staying in control, that we cannot count on only one thing going wrong at a time. It did so, using a traditional canine non-verbal method, sinking its teeth into my hamstring. A moment of searing pain gave way to a mindful grace in which I thought, "Ah, so this is what it feels like to be bitten by a large dog."

I did not catch the dog's name, although Demon Spawn briefly crossed my mind. My thigh was swelling like Jacob's after his famed angelic wrestling match, so maybe this dog was not demon but angel, delivering me the message that it was time for me to humble up. And sure enough, I found myself back at the Memorial Hospital Emergency Room registration desk where they looked at me, puzzled, still remembering my colorful arrival with my mother a handful of days earlier and not understanding why I was back in the waiting room. My sister came down from Mom's bedside to meet me there and wondered aloud whether she ought to just fill out her own emergency admission paperwork now, just in case.

I got good care, antibiotics, Percocet, and a clean bill of health. I also got, unexpectedly, an afternoon of relief from the muscle spasm I'd been experiencing in that very thigh, not unlike a bee sting relieving arthritis. And I got a lesson, a thankfully non-fatal lesson, that anything can happen. That this life unfolds in messy ways, even if we're blessed that some of it unfolds well. Staying on top of things is not possible and not desirable either. It won't keep the pain away or make the catastrophe un-happen. Instead maybe, we are condemned – or privileged – to struggle. To slog through the messes and the sadnesses and to rejoice at the celebrations that don't always quite make up for the pain, but that deserve all our love anyway. All we can do is learn to roll with the unexpected, without regard to what we will *do* about it. To be, as Berrine, a wise woman of our congregation always reminded me, a human being, not a human doing.

I learned all this from the Universe, from an angel, whose teeth and slobber I can still feel. It could have been worse. Oh wait, it was worse, just a week before, when I arrived at the ER with my mother, who was losing her motion and her words. And oh wait, that could have been worse too, and eventually it was.

We all live through hard times. And hard times are ultimately bigger than our optimism, our pessimism, or our managerial skills. The trick, I guess, is just to be open. My life contains blessing without measure. And because time is uncontrollable, unmanageable, the pearls that come – a smile, the squeeze of a hand, the arching of an eyebrow – are even more precious, each one deserving of attention and admiration.

Queer Medicine for Dark Times

Every so often, the New Moon falls the day immediately following Shabbat. That means the Sabbath falls in the darkest moment of the lunar cycle – a night with no moon at all, an utterly dark night except for whatever a clear night's Milky Way can offer. This special Shabbat has a name. It is called *Shabbat Machar Chodesh*. *Machar Chodesh* means "tomorrow is the new moon." And yes, this is a meaningful thing in the Jewish telling of time, in a way that we children of electric lights perhaps cannot fully grasp.

When Shabbat falls on the dark day before the new moon, it disrupts our ritual. On such a Shabbat the expected weekly *haftarah* portion is rejected and replaced with an excerpt from the First Book of Samuel, Chapter 20. On such a Shabbat, the entire Jewish world, no matter how progressive or how conservative, reads the queerest story of the Hebrew bible – the love affair of Jonathan and David.

Why this portion? Not because of its plot or its characters. Not because it has some special symbolism. The rabbis of antiquity slated this portion for *Shabbat Machar Chodesh* because in its opening verse, Jonathan turns to David and says, *machar chodesh*. "Tomorrow is the new moon." That's the whole tie-in. A biblical product placement for the coming new moon. I am mystified at how the rabbis thought this was a good idea. But I am delighted they did, forcing us, every once in a dark moon, to read this steamy, suspenseful story of same-sex love.

Jonathan is the son of King Saul, the first king of Israel. David is his lover, eventually to be the second king of Israel. In my experience, whenever Jonathan and David are mentioned in a Jewish space, it quickly devolves into a were-they-or-weren't-they conversation, usually pressed by someone who says they weren't. I don't feel the need to debate; the text speaks for itself. They are in love with each other. They are so into each other. Their love burns all the hotter because it is a forbidden love – not because they are both men (or not *only* because they are both men) but because Jonathan's father, King Saul, hates David and (correctly) sees him as a threat to his throne.

Shakespeare could not have done better in setting the stage. Jonathan is prepared to give up everything for David. He tries to shield him from the king's wrath and help him escape his reach. He does this, risking his own safety and his father's favor. Jonathan and David make their plans in the dark of night. Their breathless conversation could easily be scripted for Romeo and Juliet, or Tony and Maria. And, like Tony and Maria, they swear a secret oath to each other. They say, *Hineh Adonai beyni u-veyncha ad olam.* "May God witness this promise between us forever." Or maybe, "May God be in the space between us." These words are pretty much as close to a wedding vow as we see in Torah, second only to Ruth's very queer oath to Naomi.

When King Saul perceives that his son Jonathan has helped David escape, he flies into a rage, screaming cruelties at his son, and Jonathan storms out. The two lovers meet up secretly one more time before David goes into exile. This is not a dispassionate, handshake meeting. Instead, at this rendezvous, it says poetically:

Vayishku ish et-re'ehu. Vayivku ish et-re'ehu.
"They kissed each other; and they cried with each other."

Then they part, once again repeating their vow, saying, "May

God be witness to the oath between you and me, and between my seed and yours."

And that's it. Their story starts earlier; their story continues further. But this is the snapshot that we get on *Shabbat Machar Chodesh*. We see them at perhaps the darkest point in their story, just like this Shabbat is the darkest point in the month.

They don't get their happy ending. But today that's not our problem, because on *Shabbat Machar Chodesh* that's not our text. Whatever sly rabbi slated this story for this moment and chose its parameters wanted us to walk away from it with a sense not only of danger but of possibility too. For that sly rabbi, the kisses and the tears and the promises were the point.

So maybe this darkest-before-the-dawn story is the medicine for dark moments, when vengeful and erratic tyrants are pressing, when we are made to feel like outlaws, when we see the danger in fleeing and a different danger in staying, when it seems like all options are closing in on us. This is the medicine. It is queer medicine. It is love medicine.

Here is the prescription. Do like David and Jonathan: dare to love. Dare to love even when love is a transgression; *especially* when love is a transgression. Love the people you are told to hate. The stranger, the poor, the people who look different from you, the people who pray differently from you, the people who exert claims to the same land/story/privilege as you. Love each other, cry together when needed, commit to each other, for the wellbeing of the future that we are sowing. This is radical and simple. This is transgressive. This is the queer medicine for a dark time.

This special Shabbat is not called *Shabbat Choshech*, the Shabbat of Darkness. It is *Shabbat Machar Chodesh*. The Shabbat of Imminent Light. Tomorrow is the new moon. Tomorrow there will be light. Tomorrow will come renewal. Tomorrow there will be something new we haven't thought of yet. I insist on being heartened rather than hardened. Perhaps that is the explicit message of this Shabbat. When things seem darkest, the new light, the new era, is coming. *Machar chodesh*. Tomorrow the light. Count on it.

How to Find God

How to find God?

Stand at the Holy Tent in your white tunic,
hemmed in bells and pomegranates.
Recite the words you have learned.
Go to the woods and call out.
Trace a Hebrew letter on the back of your hand.
Speak names of angels and ancestors.
Look at the stars.
Smell jasmine or rosemary.

Take a walk into the unknown.
Follow a goat to a burning bush
or a calf into a cave filled with the light of Eden.
Mourn. Grieve. March.
Swim in a mountain stream.
Dunk three times.
Look in the eyes of a beloved.
Laugh with friends.
Be present. Be prepared.

Ask God how to find God.
Offer your yearning on an altar of surrender.
Lie on the grass.
Close your eyes.
Remember back to before
you came into this world.

The Theology of the Cubs

In October of 2016, I sat down with my Israeli brother-in-law and watched the Chicago Cubs win the pennant and qualify for the World Series. In the process I had to explain to him why this was significant and confront my own inner, long-suppressed fan.

I grew up with a rabbi who regularly used baseball references in his sermons. I adored Mark Shapiro, and his outfield metaphors were usually just right. That said, he was a native South Sider and a White Sox fan. Even as a kid I knew to look at his baseball enthusiasm with skepticism. Sox fans were not like Cubs fans. My family – generations of North Siders – were proud Cubs fans. Being a Cubs fan was as essential to who we were as being Jews, Chicagoans, Earthlings. We shared something special and foundational with other Cubs fans. It was different from just being a baseball fan. Cubs fans had their own kind of faith, their own special theology.

I was raised into this religion from birth. My grandfather, Joe Newman, and his brothers-in-law were all formidable Cubs fans. Every summer Sunday of my childhood, like clockwork, like Shabbos, Grandpa Joe and Grandma Sade would pull up in their Oldsmobile and we would watch the ball game together. We'd turn on WGN at 1 pm, in time to settle in with the announcers' pre-game chatter. My mother would pour her father a scotch. I'd sprawl on the floor in front of the TV, and the game would start. My grandfather, like so many Chicago grandfathers, would yell at the umpires, yell at announcer Jack Brickhouse, yell at manager Leo Durocher. Sometimes there were double-headers, and all six of us would have to eat dinner on snack tables so as not to miss any plays.

We were faithful fans although not fanatics. But fanatics did exist in my bloodline. My grandfather's uncle, Morris Levin, was a beloved figure at Wrigley Field. He earned a mention in the 1930 edition of *Ripley's Believe It or Not* for attending every game of the season and knowing every statistic in the National League, despite being blind. The players would say, "Hello, Mr. Levin" to him on their way onto the field, and he could tell from the sound of bat meeting ball exactly where a hit was headed.

Cubs games were daytime diversions in the days of my childhood; Wrigley Field had no lights. Too many extra innings and a game could be called on account of darkness, and who needed night games anyway? For Cubs fans, part of the joy was skipping school or work to go sit in the bleachers. To a Cubs fan's eye, there was something vulgar about night games. Under electric flood lights, the White Sox looked like a Vegas stage show. Real baseball took place under the blue sky and blazing sun.

I guess I say these things to try to convince you, dear reader, that I'm not just jumping on a Cubs bandwagon, even though here I am strapped in and ready to go. Baseball was, I think, something I sacrificed in growing up and coming out. In perfecting my new, rebellious, gay identity, I adopted an outspoken and derisive ignorance of sports. It was mostly true – I know nothing about basketball, football, hockey. I only care about soccer teams when they make beefcake calendars.

But baseball? I know the rules. I once knew the players. I know the pace, the feel, and the culture. When I moved to California, that spirit chilled in me. I attended a few Giants games and a couple of A's games. The company of my season ticket-holding buddy, Emily, was wonderful, but I walked into Candlestick Park, and it wasn't Wrigley Field. It was the wrong team in the wrong place, and rooting for a team that could actually win felt oddly meaningless, because being a Cubs fan has something to do with faith. Not faith in a specific outcome, but faith for its own sake. Faith as practice.

The Cubs last won a World Series when my Grandpa Joe was 5 years old. By the time I was watching ball with him 60 years later, the organizing principle of fandom could not have been any realistic expectation of winning. Instead, faith was a posture, a relationship with the world, or at least the world of baseball. Rooting for a team that had a good chance of winning was easy, and it was beneath us. That kind of fandom was for people from other cities, where strength of character was not strictly required. The theology of the Cubs fan had something to do with an embrace of the "is," rather than the "might be." It was belief without proof. Endurance without promise of reward. Patience just because.

If only we could live our lives this way! With such constancy. With exquisite endurance, faith that doesn't flag, joy even in the waiting. Holding the world – and each other – with love and loyalty, despite imperfection, despite unfinishedness. We don't need a perfected world; we don't need a perfect partner, perfect children, perfect self. If we could just hang onto life, with all its ups and downs, with the fierce love with which Cubs fans hang onto baseball, what a world this would be! And if every century or so, there's a World Series title, no one would complain.

Last Saturday, I watched the last National League playoff game, Cubs vs. Dodgers. Without a TV, without cable service, I connived my way onto the live stream. I sat, prodigal that I was, with my Israeli brother-in-law, who had never seen a baseball game, and I elaborately explained it all. The rules. Why innings don't have a timer. How a normal game lasts as long as a movie, but a memorable game with extra innings is like an opera. Why all the spitting (I had to make this one up) and crotch adjustments (ditto). What makes baseball fans better people. Pointing out how casual and respectful opponents are with each other. I felt all my love for the Cubs – not for these particular players, who were new to me and all born long after my last visit to Wrigley Field, but my love for this religion that is the Cubs.

I relaxed in a deep way, a way that encompassed my entire life and not just that moment on the sofa. I forgot my work. I forgot the fatigue from the recent High Holy Days. I forgot the awful election. It was the sixth day of Sukkot, when we call in the biblical Joseph to be our guest in the Sukkah. Instead, it was my Grandpa Joe who was clearly at my side, his scotch in hand, in answer to my glass of Sonoma merlot.

Tonight, I settle in for the World Series. Sure, I'd like us to win, but it doesn't really matter. We want it, but we don't need it. We deserve it and so do the people of Cleveland, who have been waiting a lifetime as well. We'll be fine either way because that's who Cubs fans are. That is our theology. We love, we believe, and we do so without proof or promise of reward. Now play ball.

Angels & Airports

A while back I became ill on an airplane. I guess it was a kind of extreme motion sickness. As my sister can vividly attest, I have been prone to car sickness my whole life. Planes do not usually affect me, but the van ride to the airport does. I foolishly ignore it, thinking it's nothing, but instead it incubates during the flight until it is much, much worse. By the time that happens, I am generally too delirious to understand what is going on.

So it was on my way home from Chicago. Three hours into the flight, I became ill, and when I say "became ill," I mean it as a euphemism. I became ill on the plane, luckily making it to the restroom in time. I had a naive hope that would be the end of it, but when we began our turbulent descent, I knew I was wrong. I held it together through landing but as others deplaned, I grabbed my second air sickness bag and lunged into the restroom and became ill. It was an insistent ill, a coercive ill, to which all I could do was surrender.

I emerged back into the empty plane, picked up my backpack, thanked the worried flight attendants, and tottered up the jetway. As I entered the busy terminal, I realized that the light, noise and movement of people were too much. All I could think about doing was lying down and closing my eyes. I fled the people, like a cat finding a dark place to die, and lay down on the floor.

At some point I remembered to call my husband to say I couldn't get on the bus, and that I wasn't even certain how I'd get out of the terminal. He got to work finding a cavalry of San Francisco friends to rescue me. Meanwhile, I wasn't feeling any better. In fact, I was getting worse again. I knew that if I sat up, I would *become ill*, and I realized with shock and regret that I had left the plane without grabbing a new airsickness bag.

My fevered brain struggled to chart a way out of this predicament. From my supine position, I called to a passerby, explained I was ill and asked if she could get me a bag. Getting a bag was the only next step I could imagine, the prerequisite to any other plan. She said yes and walked away, but like Noah's raven, never came back. I called to a second person that I needed help, and could he get me a bag? Off he went, returning with water (which was thoughtful) and a nut bar against dehydration (which was far beyond anything I could assimilate mentally or physically). But no bag.

When he asked if he should get me some help, I said yes. Soon, a skycap marched up with a wheelchair, cheerfully instructing me to hop in. I, still flat on the ground, said, "If I get in the wheelchair, I will *become ill*. Can you please just hand me an airsickness bag?"

"No," he smiled, "we don't have airsickness bags."

"Well, can you get me one?"

"No, those belong to the airlines," he replied, launching into a dissertation on the division of duties and materials between airline and airport, an explanation so lengthy and unwelcome that I thought I would lose it right there listening to him. When he had finally exhausted his topic, he asked if he should call paramedics.

At first, I said no. I knew what was wrong. I knew it was something that would eventually get better. I felt undeserving of a heightened level of help, but then I took stock. I was lying on the floor of an airport, unable to move. "Yes, call the paramedics," I said.

After words with his dispatcher, he told me he would wait with me. Still desperate, still foreseeing what could happen at any moment, I begged him. "You see the Peet's Coffee over there? Could you just go and get me an empty cup? When the paramedics move me, I will *become ill*. Just an empty cup please!"

He thought it over for a moment and agreed. Off he walked. My half-opened eyes followed him across the terminal. He nearly made it to Peet's, then turned around and walked all the way back. His face was earnest and helpful as he asked, "What size?"

Maybe that's enough of this story. Maybe you don't need any more details. You don't need to hear about the cup – alas, a clear plastic cup. Or about the paramedics offering play-by-play commentary to each other on every humiliating moment that followed. Or about the wheelchair rattling over the uneven tiles. Or the luggage, the car ride, or my recovery.

Enough. I'm not telling this to get your sympathy. It was a passing thing; I got better. I'm sure you have experienced things this bad or worse. And while it makes a funny story, it was not fun. It was not noble. Or romantic. Or spiritually elevating.

The point is this: in that moment, all I could do was *be*. I couldn't talk or text or think. I was the entire Universe. The Universe was 5'11" long and shaped like me. I was me being ill. I was the Universe being ill. I was a complete unity of body and soul, individual and whole, prostrate on grey carpet under fluorescent lights.

This discrete experience of suffering was, in a real way, a kind of *hineini* moment. *Hineini*, "here I am," the complete presence and complete surrender that Abraham and Moses modeled when they were called by God and responded with the single word *hineini*. We talk cheerfully in the progressive Jewish world about *hineini* moments as if they are always delightful experiences of elevated consciousness. but *hineini* moments might be more likely to happen in moments of such distress that surrender is your only choice.

It took me days to feel like myself again. I felt vulnerable and sad. Sad because I began to think about the people who come to see me in my office because of, or in anticipation of, their own suffering. People who are about to enter chemotherapy and will soon feel like I was feeling at the airport. People dealing with death or loss of myriad variety. They come to me for spiritual support, since that is what I am purportedly qualified to offer. Sometimes, I suggest that they imagine rallying Divine support, perhaps through inviting and imagining angels accompanying them to their chemo sessions.

This is what I do, and people are grateful. But I became sad realizing that as I was lying on the floor of the airport for well over an hour, a prayer never crossed my lips. Not a single angel was invoked. Not a word to God in any form, gender, or language. It wasn't that I considered it and decided against it. *It simply never occurred to me*. I was too wrapped up in breathing my next breath. This realization was hard. I felt like a failure, a fraud. I've dreamed up a spiritual cosmology and practice for myself, and when I needed it most they went straight out the jetway.

I told a trusted teacher how I hadn't thought to employ a single tool in my rabbinic toolkit. She said, "But you're not expected to do that when it's you who is in trouble. It's not something people can do for themselves."

Rabbi Shohama reminded me of a text we had studied together years ago. It's a story from Talmud about Rabbi Yochanan – a famous rabbi known for his intellect, great good looks, and ability to speak the language of trees. In the story, Rabbi Yochanan was visiting a sick student of his. He asked the student, "Is your suffering dear to you?" He didn't ask if the student's *illness* was dear to him, but rather if his suffering was. Was the student so trapped in the meaning and identity arising out of his illness that he could not imagine himself well? The student answered that no, his suffering was not dear to him. Rabbi Yochanan then bade him to take his hand and he stood him up out of the bed. The passage carefully refrains from saying that Rabbi Yochanan cured him of his disease, but something shifted that allowed the sick student to shed some of the suffering.

Fast forward in the story, and now Rabbi Yochanan himself is ill. His own teacher, Rabbi Chanina, comes to him and asks if his suffering is dear to him. Rabbi Yochanan says no, and Rabbi Chanina takes his hand and raises him up out of the bed.

Talmud then asks the obvious question: if Rabbi Yochanan had the ability to raise his student up, why didn't he just raise himself up when he was sick? Talmud answers its own question: "A prisoner cannot free himself from prison." Suffering can be a kind of prison, and a suffering person cannot be expected to unlock their own shackles. This is why in Jewish tradition we have the custom of *bikur cholim*, of visiting the sick. According to Talmud, the simple act of visiting, of being present, of witnessing, can eliminate 1/60th of a sick person's pain. And just as a sick person's suffering can only be lifted with another person's help, so I felt my teacher now lifting some of my suffering in a way that I had not been able to do for myself.

There was still something bothering me. I felt embarrassed. Not in front of my teacher but in front of the angels. At this point in my life, I take angels more seriously than I did when I was younger. I don't have a big theology or cosmology about it; I recognize that angels serve as a way of experiencing the Divine when the Divine is too big or impersonal or abstract to get what we need. I don't have set ideas about them. I don't require them to have physical morphologies or literal dimensions, personalities or plot lines. I am open to them being natural forces or human intuitions or moments of expanded consciousness or simply abstract qualities – love, compassion, care, protection – which in our imagination get embodied and beautifully robed in angelic garb. But even after all those disclaimers, let me say that I do in fact invoke angels. I call them in at bedtime as is our Jewish custom. I call them in at the beginning of a journey or a difficult project, when I'm wrestling a slippery sermon, or when I simply need some extra courage. But in that moment on the airport floor, I hadn't done it. I did not call out. And now, I felt like if I invoked angels for anything, I would be exposed and judged for my faithlessness.

My teacher suggested that I not assume; that I ask them instead. We quieted for a moment. I closed my eyes and before I could consciously formulate a question, I heard the words, "It's okay, we were there anyway." I heard the words clearly, in my ears or maybe just in my head. I felt tears of relief. Relief to know that Divine love, the Universe's care, is not conditional, and our suffering is not a test of faith. Illness happens, pain happens, and our angels stand by us whether we call on them or not.

We are living in a time of great suffering – global suffering. Our Earth is ailing, and we are not separate from it. In our roots, in our bones, in our dreams, we hear the planet's cries of distress. They color our experience of everything. They fuel our grief. They hasten our anger. They drive us to compassion or to the opposite. Whatever pain we already feel in our bodies, in our relationships, or in our body politic – that pain is heightened by the relentless groan of the suffering Earth.

But in this suffering there is the possibility of *hineini* moments – moments of deep, all-encompassing presence. Not for the fun of it but to connect us deeply with the Universe that we are. To feel its needs and its instructions so that we can be empowered to act courageously. So that we may choose life when there is a choice to be made. So that in the face of suffering, we can drop in and say *hineini*. Here I am. I am the Universe too.

Hineini. With our mere mindful presence, we can, as Talmud suggests, relieve a tiny bit of the pain that we witness. One sixtieth. It might not sound like a lot, but it's not nothing. And we can feel confident that even in our own moments of despair, in moments that we can't see our way out of the box that we're in, the angels are there anyway.

If we are the Universe, then we are the Universe in the form of someone lying on an airport floor. And in the form of someone at a border crossing. And in the form of an animal fleeing extinction. We are the Universe in the form of perky skycaps, nimble paramedics, poets, painters, and helpers of every sort. We are the Universe in the form of suffering, but also the Universe in the form of help and healing.

So take heart. We've got this. We have each other. And the Universe has us. And the angels? They've been here all along. Just look around.

Journey of Return

There's a folk story many of us know from the *1001 Nights*, but we also get it in a Chasidic retelling from Rebbe Simcha Bunem of Pshichta. In that version, we meet Rabbi Isaac of Krakow, who dreams that there's a treasure waiting for him buried under a bridge in Prague. After having this dream numerous times, he sets out to find it. When he reaches Prague and is scoping out the site, he is approached by an official who asks him what he's doing. Rabbi Isaac tells him about the dream, and the official scoffs. "Well, I had a dream also, that there is a treasure under a tile in the kitchen of someone named Rabbi Isaac in Krakow, but you don't see me upping and leaving!" Sure enough, Rabbi Isaac returns home, pries up the tile under his stove, and finds treasure.

I thought about this story as I stood on a rainy hilltop in south-western Germany at the grave of my great-great-grandfather and namesake, Isaak (or Yitzchak) Keller. I was there responding to an invitation issued to me in dreams over many years – a recurring dream in which I'd get on the wrong plane, or we'd have mid-flight mechanical difficulties, and we'd always end up landing in Stuttgart. Why? Stuttgart was a place I had no connection to, other than knowing its name through the standard redaction of the Hebrew bible known, burdensomely, as the *Biblia Hebraica Stuttgartensia*. I'd had that dream periodically for decades. Then it slackened off. But suddenly it returned just as I was planning a trip to Israel and considering a stopover in Europe.

On the merit of this dream, I bought a ticket to Germany, determined to visit Stuttgart at last and see what treasure was there for me. It was not meant to be a family history trip because I knew of no ancestors from there. Besides, the origins of all branches of my family were accounted for, with the pesky exception of the Kellers themselves, whom I'd never been able to trace back across the ocean.

The immigrant in that case was my great-grandfather, Herman Keller. He arrived in the US in the 1870s and left in his wake a discontinuity in the transmission of our history, a breach in memory. Perhaps not intentional because transmission requires both a transmitter and a receiver. Both must be powered up, working, and willing. In his case, they were not. His grandchildren – my father, my uncle, and their cousins – had no clue where their grandfather had come from. Guesses ranged from Bavaria to Hamburg to the Black Forest. The last of these, sounding most like a fairy tale, was the closest to correct.

I bought my ticket and made my plans. Days from departure, I had another dream in which my great grandfather suggested a new avenue of search. I woke up and in a series of rapid-fire internet discoveries, I found where Herman Keller (born, I discovered in that moment, Gavriel Hirsch Keller) came from, and that his parents' graves and his grandparents' graves were intact on a hilltop in Germany, a few miles from what turned out to be the town of their birth, and less than an hour from Stuttgart. This is the place I visited. No, let me rephrase that. This is the place I returned to because it felt like a journey of return. Maybe a part of it was learning that I shared a Hebrew name not only with my own Grandpa Irwin, but with his grandfather, Isaak Keller, and his grandfather, Rabbi Yitzchak, before the name Keller was adopted. The Consolidated Union of Yitzchak Kellers had launched from here, crossed the ocean to America, and now boomeranged back.

The sensation of return was reinforced by how I felt in the

surroundings. Seeing the landscape, seeing the town the Kellers came from with its half-timbered houses, I felt an unexpected comfort, where I had only expected to feel alienation. Maybe it was from childhood jaunts to excessively Teutonic Milwaukee or the porcelain miniatures of German houses in my grandmother's china cabinet. Maybe it was mystical or epigenetic or entirely born of my own overactive imagination. But whatever caused it, the surroundings felt familiar, as if I knew the language of the trees and hills and houses, even when I faltered at the language of the people.

In one version of this story, this could have been a tale of reconciliation – an American Jew in Germany to heal the violence and trauma of the past. But I didn't have any specific reconciliation to do while here – at least none that I knew of consciously. My ancestors had not been routed out or rounded up. They left for a better life in a New World, nearly as far before Kristallnacht as we are after it – a better life which, I suppose, I am now living.

Instead of reconciliation, my journey felt like a simple need to report in. I stood at those graves and announced myself in a child's German. I recited the lineage that connected us. I reported on the state of their family in America 140 years later, as best as I knew it. After I was done, it became very quiet. I began to feel the vastness and loneliness of this graveyard and a different purpose rose in my heart: I had returned so that I could witness.

These people had erected stone markers facing not toward Jerusalem but toward the future. The stones stood vigil waiting for the future to look back and see them. And in the meantime, we forgot where we came from – until German academics surveyed the stones, and later academics posted an index on the Internet just in time for some shlub in California, with nagging dreams and a plane ticket, to discover his ancestors' names and the addresses of their graves.

The people buried here wanted to be witnessed. If there was a dramatic reconciliation, it was not with Germany or the Shoah, but with the failure of memory itself. My return was a return from amnesia.

Meanwhile, even for them, things had changed. This hilltop in Waibstadt is now called the *Waldfriedhof* – the Woodland Cemetery. When the Jews began burying their dead there at the end of the 17th Century, it was a sunny, open meadow. It remained sunny and open until the last burial, in 1938. But now? Now, European sycamore maples push right up out of the graves, tilting the monuments and covering the whole place in leafy canopy. Untended, undisturbed, this bit of Jewish land gave birth to something beyond its intention. A natural forestland emerged – dark, lush, full of the trilling of birds and the shushing of leaves. A deep, shaded place beloved by hikers. The founders of the cemetery had not signed up for a reforestation project, but like all of us eventually, they surrendered to the future. Maybe my renewed dreams were a call to come now, before all sign of them would be lost, as they continued to metamorphose, Daphne-like, from Jews to trees.

I visited in one of the last possible moments in which my desire to know and their desire to be known could meet. Generations ahead might have an academic interest, if that, but probably not this investment in the particularity, and perhaps no guidance from dreams. I showed up in time, visited my ancestors and all the people they knew, so we could catch a glimpse of each other.

Sort of like that folk story of Rabbi Isaak of Krakow. Sometimes we must make the long journey to gain the perspective to see our own treasure. As I stood in the forest cemetery, I looked at the gravestones and what I saw were people looking forward into the future. All I had to do was follow their gaze in order to rediscover myself.

We completed a circuit together, those people and I. I was a *malach* – a messenger, an angel – from the future they had launched. And they became angels for me, helping me notice where I've come to, who I am, what I carry with me. I sometimes still hear their voices, full of curiosity, in my dreams at night. Curiosity and the reminder to stop right where I am and pry up a tile from the floor, where I am nearly certain to find treasure.

Postcard from the *Effeminati*

The Chicago Assyrian Dictionary is less a reference book than an epic. The project was launched in the 1920s on the back end of the great greedy wave of European exploration and colonization that swept the Near East. The dictionary was completed twenty volumes later, in 2010, by the sweat and eyestrain of generations of scholars. It cracked open old Assyrian, an eastern Semitic language of Mesopotamia, and the culture that expressed itself through it. To be a graduate student in Near Eastern languages at the University of Chicago in the 1980s was to be a cheerleader for, and witness to, the unfolding, one word at a time, of the language of Nebuchadnezzar.

I own two volumes of the dictionary, orphans that materialized on the shelf of a local used bookstore in those years. *Treasure*, I thought, spying them priced inadvertently cheaply. They were the volumes I and K – my initials! – so stumbling upon them felt *bashert*: these two heavy volumes were mystically tied to me. I spirited them home and reached first for the K volume. It fell open of its own accord to the word *kulu'u*. I leaned in close:

Kulu'u. Actor, member of the temple-personnel (of Ishtar), performing dances and music.

In those days I was not yet a performer, but the idea of dancing and singing in religious ritual sounded plenty appealing. I continued reading the entry, scanning the list of appearances of the word in ancient writings, until I hit this one:

Ša taqbû umma ku-lu-'-u la zikaru šû...

Which was translated: "He is a *kulu'u*, he is not a (he-)man."

I stopped short, looking around me, as if the dictionary were my personal tarot reading because I was also not a (he-)man. My childhood was spent as a sissy, a girlyboy. In my childhood play, I nearly always imagined myself a girl. When I was old enough to manage it, I would secretly try on my mother's dresses, her earrings, her makeup, her powder-blue high-heels. I already knew that this kind of play had to be kept secret. I had gotten caught at age 5 playing house with a neighbor boy; he was the husband and I the wife. We would kiss each other hello and goodbye. I saw nothing wrong with it until my father, regretfully I think, took me aside to tell me it wasn't allowed.

I remained whoever I truly was on the inside, while a new awareness of gender norms and their compulsory nature forced me to mimic the trappings of maleness. Junior high was a lengthy and futile campaign to walk like a boy, cross my legs like a boy, carry my books like a boy. I knew that ridicule or worse was the punishment for failing at this enterprise – and fail I did. My difference was obvious to anyone with even a modestly discerning bully's palate. When they called me "sissy," I knew they were right. I suppressed the sissy in me; I felt compassion for her but I couldn't let her out – for her own good.

It wasn't until I hit my 30s that she was allowed to pour forth in all her creativity and cleverness. It was the early 1990s. I was a graduate of Queer Nation, with its liberating slogans. "Unleash the Queen" was a popular sticker we'd wear on our ironically butch leather jackets. A few years earlier I had seen with my own eyes members of the Radical Faeries engaging in civil disobedience – men with beards, skirts, glitter and army boots, sitting in a circle on the steps of the US Supreme Court until carted off, one by one, by gloved police. What they were doing, protesting the shockingly gay-hating ruling in *Bowers v. Hardwick*, was holy work. They were shamans and they knew it. *Kulu'u*, I muttered, looking at them with admiration.

I became increasingly re-acqainted with this inner life, this *neshomeh* that had never bought into the "man" thing and was waiting for a chance to be at the wheel. When my friend Ben asked me to come to a concert in drag, and the idea for the Kinsey Sicks, later dubbed "America's Favorite Dragapella Beautyshop Quartet," was hatched, I was ready. I became a character known as Winnie, and I played her for 21 years. But "playing her" is a little misleading. I *was* Winnie for 21 years. In her shoes, in her dresses and wigs, I had the chance to be me. Certainly, she had scripted words and storylines and lyrics. But moving naturally in those heels, I was giving expression to a part of myself long awaiting her turn. I felt more at home and more honest as Winnie than I ever had in a business suit.

This was not explicitly spiritual work. I was not a *kulu'u*; not a priestess in a temple of Ishtar. On the other hand, there I was, singing, dancing, moving energy, raising consciousness, wielding whatever I could access of the feminine in a way that grabbed at the the spirit of the people in the room.

Some of my favorite moments as Winnie were off stage. If we had done a family-oriented show, which we sometimes did, mothers would bring me their babies and little children to greet and hold after the show. I was suddenly, for a moment, an honorary grandma. These moms came seeking a kind of implicit blessing – that their children be safe and whole, should they turn out to be queer. At least that's how I understood it, and I offered that unspoken blessing. I was grandmother and priestess, without it being a joke, without having to wink about it to preserve someone's gender binary. I simply was, and what I was doing was what I was meant to be doing.

Something else happened in the 1990s. I became part of a Queer Minyan in the San Francisco Bay Area. The group was heavily influenced by both the Jewish Renewal movement and Neo-Paganism. Many of the women practiced some form of Wicca, and almost all the men had been Radical Faeries. It became our custom, among the supposed men, to wear skirts for Shabbos and Yontiff when we were together. This became my enduring practice, whether with them or not. And when, in my late 40s, I began to work as a rabbi, albeit not yet ordained, I would from time to time wear a skirt on the *bimah*, so people could see me as I see me. It was not without self-consciousness, but I knew that the cause of honesty was important.

While wearing my Shabbos skirt, I sometimes like to imagine my Litvak foremothers who, slogging through *shtetl* mud, would also have been wearing heavy boots – not unlike the Doc Martens that, Radical Faerie style, always anchor my girly outfits. I imagine my foremothers, but I don't exactly embody them; I'm not playing at being them. Not long ago, a colleague saw me *davening* in boots, shirt, vest, *kippah*, *tallit*, and skirt. She referred to it later, unironically, as my "priestess getup." It's not what I had been consciously going for, but it instantly felt right. I felt honored to have been seen in a priestess way. My mind wandered back to the *kulu'u*, and I noticed some electrical charge running through the ages between them and me.

Maybe priesthood, or priestliness, is meant for my kind after all. Maybe priesthood is in fact meant for all of us. In Exodus 19:6, just before we get to Mt. Sinai and its hundreds of requirements and heavy prohibitions, God says, "You shall be unto me a *mamlechet kohanim*, a kingdom of priests." We read this verse and we feel the potential in each of us to channel the Divine, to draw it down and direct it, fingerpainting holiness into the world.

But Torah moves from this dream of universal priesthood to the very restrictive actuality of it. Priests are to be only men. Able-bodied men of the line of Aaron. The priestly nature in all of us is replaced by a priestly profession, to which women, queers, and the disabled need not apply. The priestly potential of all people – sapped away! What happened to our priestesses that might have been? What happened to the *kulu'u* of our tradition?

Driven underground, for sure. Women who would have been priestesses instead passing on secret practices to their daughters that get labeled both affectionately and dismissively as "folk ways." But where are the *kulu'u*? Why can't I find them in our Jewish tradition? Am I still meant to feel so alone?

But wait, there they are, hidden in plain sight. In Deuteronomy 23:18, just one chapter after the prohibition on men wearing women's clothing and women wearing men's, we find: "No Israelite woman shall be a *k'deshah* and no Israelite man shall be a *kadesh*." I look at this verse and suddenly the girlyman priestess is looking right back at me across 3000 years. They are not absent from our past. They are there, and we meet them as they are being suppressed and outlawed.

The *kadesh*, which should mean "holy one" or "consecrated one," gets commonly translated in English-language bibles as "male cult prostitute" or "sodomite." Discredited, prohibited, and robbed of the beauty of their unusual gender. Even where the rabbis of antiquity focused their commentaries on what might (or might not) have been the sexual component of the practices of the *k'deshim* and *k'deshot*, there is also a lurking awareness of some kind of gender transgression or non-conformity. Onkelos, in the 2nd Century, translates this same verse into Aramaic as: "An Israelite woman shall not become a *servingman* and an Israelite man shall not become a *maidservant*." In translator Onkelos' understanding, the crime is not about sexuality or idolatry, but specifically about gender.

St. Jerome, in his 4th Century Latin translation, the Vulgate, swings both ways. Translating Deuteronomy, he calls the *kadesh* by the term *scortator* – "fornicator." But in five later occurrences he translates *k'deshim* as *effeminati*. It is hard to know if he means *effeminati* disparagingly or simply descriptively. But either way, he makes clear his understanding that it is not the sexual acts of the *k'deshim* but their effeminacy that characterizes them, and that makes them targets for the ruthlessness of religion-building kings.

These are painful texts for Jewish girlymen to read. In these passages, we see our two tribes, two lineages that we belong to – the Jewish one and the queer one – with the former bragging about stamping out the latter. Torah and associated commentary treat *k'deshim* as if they are somehow foreign, practicers of some other nation's religion, as if no such people would naturally arise within Israel. But this is clearly not true. No prohibitions on cross-dressing, no prohibition on Israelite men becoming *k'deshim* would be necessary if it were not in fact actually happening.

I look across the ages and I see my people. The *k'deshim*, the *effeminati* – who knows how they would label themselves – transgender? gender-fluid? non-binary? – if they'd been born 3000 years later? Who knows how I would have labeled myself if I'd been born just 30 years later? But I see them. I envy that they had a role, a function, a title available to them. That they could, at least at some remote moment in the past, worship and minister and make music in the name of the Divine in all their splendor. I admire their courage, insistently leading the worship of Asherah, serving the Divine Feminine, in a moment when the regime was insisting that God could only be male, and so also His priests. I cry with them as they see the Divine being narrowed down by narrow minds and the truth of their bodies and lives denied. I feel my gut clench as I imagine them routed, assaulted, killed, like sissies and transgender people even today. And like today, this being done by mobs who claim to speak in God's name.

So it is with a new-found awareness that this too is my lineage that I now step into a skirt and onto the *bimah*. To restore the role that was once there for people like me, long ago, before they were stamped out, forced to pass or to survive somehow underground. I wear my priestess getup to honor them. To embody a divinity and a humanity that are larger than any gender. To make a place for everyone.

One Shabbat night it was time for *Parashat Yitro*, the Torah portion that contains God's promise that we would be a kingdom of priests. I stood in shul in my skirt and talked about the *k'deshim*. How they were girlymen like me and how St. Jerome's word – *effeminati* – was a term that I would now happily reclaim. Staring at me from the front row was an 11-year-old I'd never met, who identified as gender-fluid, although I didn't know that during the service. At *Oneg Shabbat* they came up to talk to me. As we nibbled *challah* together, they looked up and said, "I want to be part of the society of *effeminati* too."

And the tribe is reborn.

River of Light

It was the summer of 2020, a few months into the COVID lockdown, and my husband Oren and I were on a road trip to the southwest. On our second night, at a friend's home in Boulder, Utah, we stepped outside and looked up. I thought I was seeing city lights reflected in the sky, as I would at home or almost any place I've been. When my eyes adjusted, I realized that the dazzling brightness was coming from the stars themselves. The Escalante region is an official "dark zone." There is no light from any city that can penetrate this place. Dominating the sky was a vast river of light – the Milky Way. So thick, so dense, it utterly ceased being individual points of light. It was a liquid brightness painted with a watercolor brush. Although this light was hitting my eyes for the first time, it was ancient light, arriving from who knows how long ago. It was the history of the Universe streaked across the sky.

The Book of Daniel talks about a *nahar di-nur*, a River of Fire, that pours forth from God's throne. Talmud says that every day, ministering angels are created from this river. They sing praises to God and when their song is complete, they cease to exist. This phrase, *nahar di-nur*, the River of Fire, is the common rabbinic and kabbalistic name for the Milky Way. Captured in this name is an ancient awareness that while water and fire are different elements, light – even light emanating from flame – is like water. The Hebrew word for river, *nahar*, and the Aramaic word for light, *nehora*, are nearly identical, reflecting our pre-modern ancestors' clear grasp of the shared nature of light and rivers, each simultaneously particle and wave.

That night in Utah, I bathed in the waters of the River of Light. For a little while, I was able to lay down by that riverside so much of what I had been carrying for months — fear of wildfire, fear of catastrophe, the isolation of the pandemic's early months, fear for our democracy, pain over the unceasing violence against people of color, revulsion at the rancor in all public conversations, despair at the peril to the planet itself, and the grief that runs like groundwater under our feet. For those minutes, the Milky Way, the River of Light, lifted me and drew me into a higher consciousness. The fate of the world wasn't on my shoulders; Creation was not dependent on my words, my actions, my ability to change minds or mobilize votes. For a few moments I was relocated to a part of my own existence that wasn't tied to the particulars of striving or suffering or solving. Instead, I was immersed. I was simply part of — and swimming in — the unfolding Creation itself.

In the flow of this ancient light, spiraling out from the beginning of time, I recognized the waters of Creation. In Genesis we read: *V'nahar yotzei me'Eden l'hashkot et hagan.* "A river pours forth from Eden to water the Garden."

It is easy to roll right past this verse inside the larger Creation story that Torah offers, but this verse is unusual. It is unlike all the verses before it and after it, which are written in the past tense. Those verses tell Creation as the story of something that happened and is done with. God breathed life into the human. God planted a Garden. God put the human in the Garden. Ancient, mythic acts, long complete. But this verse, the verse about the river, is not in the past tense. It is expressed with a present participle. Not "a river poured forth" but rather, *A river is pouring forth.* Our commentators and kabbalists saw in this unusual tense a hint that there is something from the Beginning, from the first burst of Creation, that is still flowing. We are still in the current of a primordial stream; the Garden is still being watered.

I love this image of ancient and continuing flow, but it's hard to feel it in a time that seems so often drained of its juice. I look at our civilization and feel the grinding of the gears. Where is the expanded consciousness, the spiritual richness, the generosity? In this dry riverbed of a time, I slog forward, parched, finding it hard to be civil, calm, brave, creative, hopeful. We are not the first generation to face tremendous danger; every era has been dire for someone. And dire times can drive us to the narrowest possible vision.

But I want to open the floodgates and be bathed again by that river from Eden! At certain moments we all perceive there is more at work in our lives than the physical particulars of our predicament. There are levels of consciousness deeper and higher than the day's headlines and they are moving in us too. We might experience them in special moments. In the first bloom of love or holding hands in old age. In hearing a symphony performed. In making art. In studying. In singing in harmony. In dancing with abandon. In offering true kindnesses. These are real moments – even if brief – in which we sometimes shift to and act from a different level of consciousness. Our hearts crack open and we feel kinship with the strangers sitting around us in the theatre or with the animals and plants with whom we just shared a walk in the woods. Maybe we experience this larger-than-human consciousness when in proximity to death or to birth. In these liminal moments, our consciousness gets altered; we receive a visceral awareness of the marvel of Life.

I want those moments, but mostly I live in the everyday world. I'm busy dressing, driving, eating, doing my job. I am disconnected from you and you from me and both of us from the more-than-human world. Days – or more – can go by without feeling any of that magical "oneness."

Torah notices that, because a moment after we read about the primordial river from Eden, the river separates into four. Separation, Torah seems to tell us, is inevitable. Yet even in the tributaries, in all the separate streams that circulate to all the far places, it is the same water that is flowing. It is still the water of the river flowing from Eden, just as all of the energy and matter making up our everyday existence are still the exhale of the Big Bang. As soon as you think of it that way, you are no longer in the world of separateness, but have been drawn back into the waters.

I will always love to look at the Milky Way, but not as something far off, unrelated to my life here on this planet. I also live in the Milky Way, in the *nahar di-nura*, the River of Light. Our planet, our physicality, our evolution, even our individual thoughts right now, are all part of that paintbrush stroke that first hit the canvas at the Beginning and is still in motion. We are part of *zohar harakia* – the radiance of the heavens. And as the Zohar says about that Milky Way radiance: "what is this expanse illuminating Earth if not the river flowing forth from Eden to water the Garden?"

We are in the River. We *are* the River. Let's dive in and swim. And if that's too big an ask, we can do what my grandmother would do at the lakeshore. She'd wade in up to her ankles, lean over, shpritz herself and say with true feeling, "What a *mechayeh*."

We are in the River of Light. What a *mechayeh*.

City of Flowers and Stone

It's less like other cities in Israel and more like Burning Man, I explain to our 14-year-old as we head to Jerusalem. It is summer of 2015, and we had stopped for a *nosh* in Herzliya at a branch of a sophisticated Israeli coffee chain, a last swig of stainless-steel modernity before beginning the climb to bewilderment that the Old Jerusalem Road has come to represent.

What I mean by being like Burning Man, I explain (since for him, a 2-time Burning Man veteran, this is a meaningful and friendly point of reference) is that everything in Jerusalem is notched up one tick. People who visit here are *tourists-plus*. People who live here – at least in Jewish west Jerusalem – are *residents-plus*. They're Seekers or Pilgrims or Professional Jews or Chasidim or Artists or Poets or Peace Workers or Little Old Ladies Who Immigrated Against All Odds. Like Burning Man, everything has intentionality. There is nothing casual. Even trying to live casually here requires a romantic idea and considerable effort. A seemingly simple life in an orderly Rechavia apartment, taking the bus to concerts, and sipping iced coffee in a corner cafe is a normalcy that must be painstakingly fashioned. Not making a statement here is itself a statement. *See? I live in Jerusalem, and I'm not a crackpot like those others.*

This city mystifies me. I arrive here each time and fail to find my way around. I lived here for a full year in college and I've had many other occasions to spend time in Jerusalem. But each time, when I roll in, the streets rearrange themselves so that I'm always walking the long way when the most direct route starts right where I'd been standing. Something I remember as next door turns out to be many blocks away – something I remember as prohibitively remote suddenly looms in front of me. Finally today, I give up altogether and leave the map in my pocket, letting our 14-year-old's best friend do the navigating, using the impressive internal compass he's somehow developed in just 48 hours.

I'm always at a loss for where I stand in Jerusalem, not just geographically. I don't know how to represent myself. I'm an American Jewish tourist, but I mostly shy away from American Jewish tourists for internalized anti-Semitic reasons that I have yet to fully own. My Hebrew is fluent, and I know a smattering of Arabic, so I prefer to be taken for an unidentifiable foreigner when possible – an international man of mystery rather than someone for whom Israel was the next expected step after summer camp.

But this is a city where people clearly represent themselves. Everyone has a specific role in the social disorder, and they wear associated uniforms to be easily identifiable to others and to each other. The height of the hat. The pattern on the scarf. Long coat. Short coat. Wig. Headwrap. White *kippah*. Leggings. My friend Amichai Lau-Lavie has stood with me in Jerusalem, pointing out passersby, identifying branch of Chasidism, city of origin in the Old Country, and specific Yeshivah based entirely on the particulars of costume. I am not so expert, and the 14-year-olds are complete novices. When I point out two dark-robed, bearded men to them in the Old City, the kids cycle through every flavor of Chasid they'd ever heard of before I explain that they are Russian Orthodox priests. I would like to wear a *kippah* here. I have a gut desire to somehow convey visually that I take my place in Judaism seriously. But I don't understand the ideological iconography of *kippot* well enough to know and control what statement I may or may not be making in the process. I also find myself uncomfortable with a display that is, in Israel at least, so deeply gendered.

Like many of the people in this city, I engage with Torah, but I don't know how to engage *with them* about Torah. I don't know the rules here, and I'm afraid of being proselytized or patronized or even – my deepest unspoken fear – bullied. Do I dare try? The Chasid next to me on the bus today coming from the Western Wall (long black coat, brimmed hat, pants-not-stockings), who keeps dozing off and falling into me, was at first trying to study this week's Torah portion, *Balak*, as I could see by covertly eyeing his reading material. Do I strike up a conversation? Do I say, *I think Balaam knew all along he was going to bless the Children of Israel; he just had some personal process and political wrinkles to work out, don't you think?*

Maybe he would be surprised and delighted, but I am afraid of scorn. So, despite *Pirkei Avot* telling us that where two people exchange words of Torah, the Divine Presence rests, I keep silent and leave a restless Shechinah hovering somewhere outside of the bus, breathing exhaust. Maybe if I could be here longer, more than a few days every couple years, I could find an entry point, a crack in the stone. This is a city of stone, after all: Jerusalem stone – the off-white limestone that every building, by custom and law, is made of, giving the city a silvery glow at night and its famed "Jerusalem of Gold" radiance by day. Out of its cracks grow scrubby, flowering things – lantana, bougainvillea, sage. Stone and flower are how this city looks; dust and rosemary are its smells.

It is also a place of blazing white heat. Not just solar heat but political heat. Ethnic heat. Religious heat. I go with the kids to the Western Wall to tour the tunnels underneath. This excavation reveals the full western side of the Roman-era Temple Mount, of which the Western Wall where Jews pray constitutes only a small fraction. To do this we breeze past the paltry women's prayer section and the much more generous men's section, aware that before the State of Israel, men and women mingled freely at this holiest of spots, while the division of the sexes is now zealously enforced by police, with the bulk of rights and privileges denied to women altogether.

We descend into the tunnels, which were mined under the 1400-year-old Muslim Quarter, and it belatedly dawns on me how this very excavation is meant, at least in part, to undermine Muslim authority in this much too holy, much too earthly place. You see, every stone here is claimed, and every claim is refuted. And so it has been since Jerusalem's earliest history. Jebusites, Israelites, Babylonians, Persians, Greeks, Romans, Muslims, Mamluks, Crusaders, Ottomans, Arabs, British, and now the tense Palestinian-Jewish standoff. We tend to imagine clean lines of ownership, like a chart in a textbook looking like a layer cake, but the struggle for Jerusalem has always been stone by stone, street by street, tunnel by tunnel, neighborhood by neighborhood. Small and constant aggressions only occasionally punctuated by outright conquest.

At the end of the tour, we reverse course and retrace the entire underground route to the Jewish-run and heavily policed Western Wall Plaza. There would be no exit today through the Muslim Quarter. The Old City was to be closed to tourists at noon because it is the one-year anniversary of Jewish hoodlums kidnapping and killing an Arab boy in retaliation for the abduction and murder of three Jewish Yeshivah boys. Everyone fears tensions will be high. Conflict hangs in the Jerusalem air like pollen, like dust, like humidity. You feel complicit by breathing it. Yet breathe you must.

But here's the thing: I still love this place. With all its intensity and problematicity, with its beyond-cliche contradictions, it's a place where uncanny things happen. Where on my first night here at age 16, I unexpectedly bumped into Mark Shapiro, my home rabbi, at the Western Wall. And today, at age 54, I bump into him again at virtually the same spot, on his 80th birthday. It is a place where I once decided to seek out the grave of Chanah Rochel Verbermacher, the near-heretical female Chasidic rebbe known as the Maiden of Ludmir, on the Mount of Olives and – would you even believe me if I told you? – as soon as I admitted I was lost and gave up, a bird sang out and then, with a series of hops from gravestone to gravestone, led me right to it.

This place is thick with the uncanny living unremarkably alongside the prosaic: dust and noise, soldiers and vendors, bus drivers and shouting children. I can't explain how this happens. Do the overlapping dreams that thousands of people bring here somehow congeal to form a thick and conductive spiritual field? Magic happens everywhere, perhaps, but here, like at Burning Man, everyone is looking for it all at once.

Clearly, life is simpler anywhere else than here. When I leave Jerusalem, I always feel a dash of sadness and a tablespoon of relief. But right now, I'm here. We welcome Shabbat with the music-making hip Jews of Nava Tehila, down at the old train station. We walk through neighborhoods that are probably quieter in my mind than they are in actuality. We hang out at a park where the two 14-year-olds, with no real knowledge of Hebrew, manage to organize neighborhood children into some wild game of intrigue. Then at some point, the light changes and the city indeed gets quieter and gentler. Snippets of Shabbat melodies pour out of windows, laughter too. A calm pervades, and the Shechinah, earlier kicked off a crowded bus, now robed in purple night, settles at last on this city of flowers and stone.

The Scent of Shechinah

In the journey in the desert,
what will you be?
Goatherd? Guide? Gopher?
Priest? Prophet? Perfumer?

There in the wilderness,
amid scrub and thorns,
to make a *mishkan*,
a holy pop-up Sanctuary
where tablets are kept
and where *Shechinah* dwells,
will you share your arts?

Your clever fingers shuttling
the fine yarns and dyes.
Making curtains and covers,
beams and basins,
and gold cherubim –
face to face,
framing the Divine face between.

Will you make it not just a feast for the eyes
but one for the nose as well?
A place for ascent through scent?

Torah gives the recipe:
Take 500 shekels of myrrh, says God,
half that much of cinnamon, a spice so old
that even in Torah it is already called *kinneman*.
Another 250 of *k'neh* – calamus root?
And 500 of *kiddah* – that's cassia,
another bark with some bite.

Grind to a pulp, Torah hints, then blend
with olive oil to make a rich balm
that is not burned but rubbed
on altar and ark, lampstand and laver,
greasing the fittings with good-smelling goop.

These are not like the fragrances of today,
chemicals cooked in corporate labs,
carrier waves for smells that might once
have had something to do with nature.
Possibly. Or maybe not even.

In this old time, in the desert,
scents were devised with sensibility.
Mortar and pestle. Delights olfactory
made of industry but no factory.
A time when the word "natural"
was not needed before "fragrance"
because what else would it be?

Things smelled of what they were.
The perfume smelled *of* cinnamon.
It did not smell *like* cinnamon,

Not like now. Not like the reek
of detergents, soaps and candles,
and air fresheners plugged into walls
and taxicab dashboards.

In the desert *Mishkan* it was simpler:
One part cinnamon, two parts myrrh,
cassia, calamus, oil.
Stir.

We never know how we'll serve until we get there.
But what if it were *you* whose job
was to make the perfume?
What if this were your service,
the product of your wise heart,
your skilled fingers,
your much maligned Jewish nose.
You, the *rokeach*, the aromatist!
You whose work is to waft
what Yahweh wants to whiff?

At the end of your long day,
crushing, stirring,
anointing all that is holy –
pans, poles and priests,
Would you come home empty-handed
as God commanded?
Or would you risk retribution
and sneak some for yourself –
A trace behind the ear?
A drop in the soft of your wrist?
As enticement for a lover.

As invitation to a dream.
As memory of Shechinah
and a reminder that you too are God.

Unlikely, Inevitable You

You were meant to read these words.

Right now as I write them I don't know your name and I can't picture your face. But you, securely in the future, can see that everything led to your reading them. Maybe someone you trust gave you this book. Maybe you are rifling through it in a bookstore, and your thumb came to rest on this page. You see? Destiny brought you here. Or screw it, maybe it was chance. It's so hard to know.

Take, for example, the story of Joseph. His is a story that is either about destiny or about chance, depending on whether you read from the beginning or from the end. I'll explain. Joseph is the son of Jacob and Rachel, who dies when Joseph is still young. As a teenager Joseph has vivid dreams, which he understands to signal that his brothers will bow down to him. Joseph is either confident or clueless enough to tell them that.

Joseph's brothers hate him with a murderous venom. While contemplating killing him, they cast him into a pit. When a caravan passes by, they sell Joseph into slavery in Egypt. There, Joseph has a series of adventures and misadventures, but as Torah puts it, "God was with him." He manages to pull himself out of slavery, interpreting Pharaoh's dreams and becoming Pharaoh's deputy. His task is to manage the collection and distribution of food during the seven years of plenty and seven years of famine that Pharaoh's skinny-cow dreams predicted.

Meanwhile, the famine has also overtaken life back home. Rumors spread that there is food in Egypt, and the older brothers are dispatched to go there and procure. There, they come face to face with Joseph – without recognizing him. After all, many years have passed, and Joseph looks and dresses and speaks like an Egyptian. He is not just any Egyptian, but one of great importance. They bow low before him, just as Joseph had dreamt so long ago. Prophecy fulfilled.

Joseph begins playing out a dangerous game with them. He treats them generously, but also threatens them if they do not return with their youngest brother, Benjamin. Once they do, Joseph frames Benjamin for theft, telling the other brothers to go home to their father while Benjamin stays on as his slave. Who knows what Joseph really intended? Who knows how the old trauma stirred in him, what anger or fear arose when he saw his abusers walk into the room? Perhaps he was just trying to get Benjamin away from them. Perhaps Joseph was trying to reveal his brothers' dark hearts to their father or to punish them with a new helping of culpability.

Whatever his specific intention, Joseph set up a test. Would they repeat what they did to him, abandoning a brother into slavery and burdening their father with a terrible loss, or would they choose another path? Could they break free from who they once were? Or was the future fated to be as the past had been?

Joseph's older brother, Judah, steps forward and makes an impassioned plea for Benjamin's freedom. Judah was the brother who so many years ago had proposed selling Joseph into slavery rather than killing him. But now he refuses to leave without Benjamin and offers himself up to be Joseph's slave in Benjamin's stead. His words are terse and emotional. Joseph can't hold back any longer. He sees the *tikkun* here – that his brothers are righting the old wrong by making a different choice now. He empties the room of servants and unmasks himself to the brothers, who stand there, blinking, bewildered.

Before they can catch their breath, Joseph says, "Do not reproach yourselves because you sold me into Egypt. It was God who brought me here so that I could save your lives and ensure your survival on earth."

Joseph repeats three times in as many verses that his ending up in Egypt was God's doing, which is a very generous thing to say to people who threw you in a pit and abandoned you to slave merchants. Does Joseph actually believe what he says? That it was all a circle being drawn and now closed? That despite what he suffered in the pit, in the caravan, in Egyptian servitude, and in a dungeon, it was ultimately for a blessing?

"Everything happens for a reason," people often say, but we don't ever know on the front end if it's true. We want our actions to have purpose, but we can't clearly see where the chains of cause and effect that we launch will land. When Joseph predicts his brothers' bowing down to him, there is no way to tell if it would happen, and if it did, what actions would bring it about. Because in any moment, anything can happen. This makes any particular outcome so unlikely.

Let's face it, *everything is unlikely*. We are unlikely. You and I are here because of the decisions our parents made, and our grandparents, and all our ancestors in an unbroken line back to the first living organism. Decisions of our ancestors and decisions made about them by others. Not just big decisions. What to have for dinner or when to take a walk all played a role. Any different decision of almost any sort, and we, as individuals, wouldn't be here.

Physician and dating guru Ali Binazir calculates that the odds against any of us being alive in this moment are something like $10^{2,685,000}$ to 1. That is 10 with almost 3 million zeros after it. And those are just the roughest possible odds since the beginning of life on earth. Back up from there to the Big Bang and add in the odds of this planet forming at all! Every single condition had to be just right.

As Dr. Binazir puts it, the odds of our being here are basically zero. We are completely unlikely. Each of us. Yet that same calculus works in the inverse when we look back. Given everything that *did in fact happen* – choices, accidents, migrations, mutations, weather events – our being here right now is the inexorable outcome. We are completely unlikely but also completely inevitable. Each of you reading this. Completely inevitable. And that paradox is huge and magical.

So it was for Joseph, and Joseph knew it. Yes, his survival was unlikely. His rise to power unlikely. The brothers' ever seeing each other again unlikely. But looking back from the moment of their reunion, Joseph could see that everything led there. Everything had to line up perfectly for all of them to be saved. This is the kind of destiny that Joseph is inspired to call "God."

The facts are the same for us. The odds against any of us are immeasurable. When we look forward, all is unlikely. When we look backward, all is inevitable. Maybe we are here for a reason, like Joseph. But it is up to us to determine what that reason is. What does the extreme privilege of existence inspire us to do? How do we use this improbable moment to up our game and this world's game? To set in motion acts of kindness or healing even though we don't know for certain where they will land?

We are all unlikely and inevitable beings, and that encourages me. I don't know if I am *meant* to be here. I don't know if you are *meant* to read this. But you and I – our being here defies all odds, and the whole of Creation led to it. So, if that doesn't give us some hope that our being here has meaning, what does?

With Scott in the Crosswalk

Scott and I met in an unspeakable way, in that way that gay men meet, or did back in the day. It was the summer of 1984, in Hyde Park, on the South Side of Chicago. He was just 24 and I was about to be. We knew right away we liked each other more than such circumstances typically warrant.

Scott had a partner, and I was on a brief hiatus from mine. With just a little clunkiness, we engineered a friendship that included them and moved forward from there. I was pleased for our above-board friendship, but truth be told, I think I was always a little in love with Scott. It was hard not to be. He was adorable, creative, funny. He was an architectural historian with a museum job. He was interested in material culture, and nothing pleased him more than a vintage Mixmaster. He appreciated my range of interests, but he was not a shlepper like me. His home was beautiful, he dressed well, he sparkled. He introduced me to the varied delights of Jean Philippe Rameau and Lisa Stansfield.

Time went on. He and his partner, Allen, moved to the North Side, to a house they renovated. One day we bumped into them at the farmers' market in Lincoln Park. Scott looked upset; he took me aside, ducking behind melons or Swiss chard to tell me he'd tested positive for HIV. In the late 1980s there were no treatments that could do any more than prolong the inevitable. The epidemic filled our lives – our time, our worry, our most dreaded imagination. Chicago didn't have numbers like San Francisco or New York, but numbers didn't matter. What was happening was happening in the heart of the gay community, to people you knew well, and people you knew across a room, and people you had smiled at at a bar. Scott had always felt to me like a sunny Chicago day, a bright hot day where everyone is out barbecuing on the lakefront, making up for a long, hard winter. But in the farmers' market that day, his face was clouded.

I'd begun to come out in 1981. The first headlines of a gay cancer and speculations that it might have a viral cause broke at the same time. My boyfriend and I had close calls. Our parents lived in fear. The terrible way gay people were thought of became visible in new ways, as gay men died by the thousands and the smiling president could not bring himself to say the word AIDS.

I joined others in protests and candlelight vigils. I ran an underground clinic in our apartment. I joined the fight for an equal rights bill in Chicago and organized protests against some of the early AIDS years' biggest villains. I went to law school thinking my people – in this case the gay people, not the Jews – needed more advocates with more skills. I moved to San Francisco and became an AIDS legal services provider until the year 2000, when the Kinsey Sicks were courted for an Off-Broadway show – the Kinsey Sicks, whose formation was itself another response to the desperate and painful time we were living in.

When Scott got his diagnosis, I already knew many who had died of AIDS. I had designed a University of Chicago panel for the Names Project AIDS quilt, with names of grad students, undergrads, faculty, and staff. But of all the people I knew, Scott was closest to me. Other losses motivated me politically, but it was Scott whose loss I could not imagine.

As happens sometimes when faced with a dire diagnosis, Scott shook up his life. He broke up with Allen and got himself a fine old Chicago apartment which he decorated tastefully and began using to entertain – theme parties with dinner menus to match. He had a black-and-white party once, featuring squid-ink pasta and white clam sauce. He dismissed my suggestion that he hang posters of Karen Black and Betty White, accusing me of mocking his very gay visual aesthetic. I probably was. I was a vegetarian, which conveniently allowed him not to invite me.

Scott ran through a couple boyfriends before settling on Victor, an aggressively showy stage actor and drama teacher, who, I thought at the time, tended to steamroll unfairly over Scott's gentler demeanor. Once Scott was in a relationship with Victor and I had moved to California, we were less in touch, although never out of touch. The two of them visited a couple times – Scott wanting to connect, Victor wanting to disrupt.

In 1994 Scott called with a proposition. He and Victor were going to Italy for three weeks. Victor wanted to spend the first ten days in his family's ancestral village, a foray that would not include Scott. Would I join him for those 10 days in Italy? I understood the subtext. This could be our last time together of any quality. Italy (and maybe I) were on his bucket list.

It was late August, a hot and dusty Saturday, when I arrived in Rome. We had timed our flights – his from Chicago, mine from San Francisco – to arrive at our *pensione* simultaneously. I struggled with buses and maps and needed the advice of Spanish-speaking Peruvian expatriates to arrive, disheveled, at the hotel. The proprietor greeted me with a fax – not a good omen. It was from Scott. He and Victor had gotten to O'Hare Airport only to discover that Scott's passport was expired. Scott kissed Victor goodbye and raced downtown to the passport office. They closed the doors behind him and would have made him a passport on the spot, if only he'd had a passport photo. But he didn't, and it was now 5 pm on Friday. They instructed him to come back Monday morning with a photo, and he could catch the Monday afternoon flight, landing him in Rome on Tuesday.

I bore my disappointment with pluck – however disappointing it was for me, it was worse for him. I moved to a cheaper hotel. I visited museums and churches. I battled jetlag and linguistic timidity. I ate *gnocchi a la gorgonzola* every day at the same *trattoria*.

At last it was Tuesday and she arrived – Miss Thing, Signorina Cosa, Scott LaFrance, homo-at-large, present and accounted for. Scott hit the ground running. There was only one day left to be in Rome before we had reservations elsewhere. Scott would be back in Rome with Victor in a week, but wanted to cram in everything I could show him. With a remarkable push I'd never seen in anyone, we visited the Pantheon, the Trevi Fountain, the Colliseum, the Forum, the Campo dei Fiori, the Piazza Navona. This was how he responded to having missed three days: by compacting them into one. Filling limited time with an over-abundance of experience was a task all too familiar to him.

Our subsequent days were a mix of delight and difficulty. He was in physical pain much of the time, often trying to hide it from me or making the best of it for himself. We ate pastas and sauces and wild mushrooms. As was his habit, he would memorialize an experience we had together by reducing it to a nickname that he could call me again and again. Delighted at a menu of side dishes, he began calling me Missy Contorni. After eating delicately fried squash blossoms, I became "my little *fior di zucca*." And when we'd inadvertently bump into each other on the sidewalk back to the hotel after eating much too much food, he'd call me Missy Bigbutt.

I didn't comment on the wincing look in his face as he pushed on through pain and fatigue. When it was too much, he would not accept defeat but would rather incorporate his fatigue into the tour. "This would be a good spot to take in a little *veduta*." So, we'd sit down on the bench or curb or ancient Roman buildingstone and look at the landscape, or the road, or the playing children, or the angle of the sunlight.

At night he'd be playful – hurling pillows at me from across the room or tickling me when I wasn't looking. Or he'd be spent. One night, ill and afraid, he looked across the room at me reading Calvino and asked, "Ir honey, would you come over and just hug me a little?" I held him as requested, feeling all my love for him, neither of us thinking beyond this moment, or at least not revealing that we were.

A year and a half later, I was spending a weekend with the Kinsey Sicks, writing a show that we were planning to put up shortly in San Francisco. It was still our early years. We spent a long day at Ben Schatz's house in Hayes Valley and then we all slept over. Tossing and turning, I dreamt myself in Chicago. It was late night, and the streets were empty. Scott and I were crossing a street in Boys Town or Andersonville, when suddenly he sank to the ground. I caught him and held him in my arms in the crosswalk. I knew he was about to die. I said over and over, "No, Scott, I'm not the one who is supposed to be with you." I called for help, but there were no reinforcements. I held him until my own wailing woke me up.

Filled with alarm, I called Chicago. Scott and I hadn't spoken in a month or two, on account of neglect and maybe dread on my part; on his part, maybe a desire not to burden me. Who knows? Victor told me that things were starting to take a turn for the worse. My next call was to the airline, and the day after next I was on a plane to O'Hare. I didn't stop to see my parents but taxied straight to Scott's apartment, where he was now in a hospital bed, having gone on hospice that day. A visiting nurse was with him, and both Victor and Allen, Scott's partner when I'd first met him, hovered, trying to pick up caregiving tips and find meaningful things to do.

Living now in Boston, Allen had been flying to Chicago 3 days a week to manage Scott's care. I wondered how Scott felt about this arrangement – he had not broken with Allen years before only to find himself dependent on his care now. Victor undoubtedly had feelings about Scott's ex taking over situation management too. But even Victor knew that the situation needed to be managed, and that management was beyond him. It was also clear that despite everything else, Allen's love for Scott was real and unabated. So Victor and Allen teamed up, an unlikely pair, each abiding the other for the sake of their, and our, shared beloved.

The next day, things looking stable, Allen gave us lists of things to do and boarded his plane back to Boston. I sat with Scott and reminisced. We watched an unsatisfying movie. I helped him in the bathroom. I puttered and tried to offer food. Scott was now getting morphine and becoming spacy. Victor was out during the day and evening teaching. He got home late, and after a few minutes alone with Scott, found me in the kitchen.

Victor had always seemed to me equal parts clown and provocateur. But now he dropped all facade in that kitchen of tasteful tile and shelves arrayed with Scott's carefully curated kitchen gadgets. He said he couldn't bear to see Scott like this but was terrified to live without him. He burst into tears and sobbed on my shoulder. We were in that posture when we heard Scott call out in alarm from the bedroom.

We rushed in. He was confused; he said he'd had an accident, but he hadn't. Maybe it was the sudden awareness of the organs of his body taking their leave. His face was fretted. As we held him, his breath calmed and then the pauses between them lengthened. I realized what was happening before Victor did, and began pouring forth endearments, telling Scott that it was okay for him to go, cueing Victor to do the same.

We didn't have long to wait. It was two in the morning when Scott let go of his beautiful earthly body, the wee hours of February 29th, Leap Day. He died on a day that, like him, is rare, and cause for notice. And in so doing he elegantly deprived his loved ones of an annual day to mark his memory. Instead, all we can do is stay up late on February 28th and greet Scott in the blink of an eye that ushers in the lion month of March.

I was grateful to be there at the end. Maybe I was the right person after all, who knows? It was so unlikely, and maybe, ultimately, inevitable. In later years I had cause to spend time with Allen, now happily repartnered, when I'd tour New England. Victor and I lost touch almost immediately, although I know that he went through a terrible cancer that left him in constant pain, and with his signature flair, he announced the end of his life and then made it happen.

There are still a few of us who continue to hold Scott's memory, alone or in pairs. I wear one of his ties, listen to a couple of his CDs, and have a painting by his grandmother in my kitchen. He's been gone more than twice the length of time I knew him, but I still sometimes feel him close. I try to imagine who he'd have been if he had aged alongside me. But when I see him in my mind's eye, he is always 35, standing under a streetlight, smiling at me from the other side of a crosswalk.

Reflections of a Retiring Drag Queen

It was Kahlil Gibran who first famously said, *if you love someone, let them go.* Which has to be the stupidest advice I've ever heard. Yes, if they don't come back, they were never yours, blah blah blah. But who wants to find *that* out? And then you're just left full of highfalutin principle, surrounded by people you don't particularly care for. No. If you love someone, hang on tight.

That's what Winnie and I did. We stuck together for 21 years. She saw me through a lot: legal practice, new love, marriage, children, the boomeranging of a long cast-off rabbinic calling, and the loss of both my parents. In return, I saw her through meltdowns, hairdos, artificial insemination, Republicanism, lesbianism, cleaning obsessions, and even prison (for trafficking in Julia Child pornography, if you must know).

But in 2014, Winnie and I, at long last, bade each other farewell. No scandal. No drama. No cheating. No vicious fight over the labradoodle. It's just that we want different things. She might nod towards domesticity, but she loves her life on the stage. I love life on the stage too, but after 21 years, I wanted to be home.

By now the story of the founding of the Kinsey Sicks is well known to those who care about such things. There was a Bette Midler concert, a little circle of friends, and a crazy idea. There was an enthusiastic if undeserved ovation from an audience full of people not there to see us. That was in December of 1993. Seven months later we were on an iconic street corner, Castro and Market, at Harvey Milk Plaza, performing our first show. I look at video of that performance and there we are, the Kinsey Sicks, sprung fully formed out of the pounding heads of Ben Schatz, Jerry Friedman, Maurice Kelly, Abatto Avilez, and me.

Well, maybe not *fully* formed, but well on our way. Rachel was already obnoxious, Trixie a slut, Vaselina a dipshit. Winnie was the one waiting to begin a long journey of self-discovery. At the beginning she emulated her mother, i.e. me, far too much. She was Irwin in a dress. I wasn't an actor; I didn't know how to create a character. I see myself in those years: bearded, wooden, engaging in some side task like finding props or adjusting someone's microphone, thinking no one would notice. As if by sheer force of will, I could make my on-stage multitasking invisible.

But luckily, Winnie began asserting herself. I confess that I liked her well enough, but I didn't start falling in love with her until maybe 7 years later. That's when I began loving her for her faults. I realized that while my own insecurity on stage and determination that nothing go wrong were an impediment to my performance, they were the stuff of sublime comedy for Winnie. Slowly, I learned that Winnie is far more entertaining in her foibles than her triumphs unless the triumph is obviously illusory. Winnie standing center-stage in wide-eyed panic, searching for a way to cover up the awful thing that the other girls undoubtedly just did, is Winnie at her funniest and her most lovable. Not just to the audience, but to me.

Like all our characters, Winnie grew to embody the traits that make me bad dinner company. Winnie would blurt out esoteric trivia – which the other girls came to refer to as *unnecessaria*, as in "Well thank you, Winnie, for that little bit of *unnecessaria*." Often, it would have to do with grammar, or subtle points about Proto-Semitic lateral fricatives. She would, with great enthusiasm, try to amuse an overdrinking Puerto Vallarta audience with a bizarre tale about Jewish-American writer Grace Paley, who, according to Winnie, once visited the nearby fishing village of Yelapa, met a man, married him, and changed her name, causing her to utter the now-famous palindrome, "A Paley Was I Ere I Saw Yelapa." Then Winnie would stand on stage in the silent, puzzled room, chuckling at her own joke, unaware that no one else was amused.

Over time, her belief in her correctness and infallibility became her stock and trade. She would brag about the cute little pet names her sweetheart called her, such as "Ouch" and "Don't." Or in a beautifully cutting Ben Schatz-written moment, Winnie would turn to the girls with authority, and begin, "Girls, is it just me?" And Trixie would reply, "Usually," before another word could be uttered.

Winnie was good medicine for me, good medicine for my tricky ego and my belief in my own infallibility. She proved to be iconic for people like me who think well of themselves, often out of fear that they're not good enough. She demonstrated that insecurity and overconfidence can co-exist and be lovable. She saved me thousands on therapy and made me a better person.

I let go of Winnie and the Kinsey Sicks for a range of reasons. Wanting to miss fewer birthdays, Chanukahs, and school plays was one. My own father was a bandleader who worked nights and weekends. I never felt his absence – he was very present when he was home. I was secretly thrilled that the kids on the block always saw him going to and from work in a tuxedo. (A sentiment that the children of my family might or might not have shared about my going to work in purple brocade.) But I know that missing much of our childhood was my father's great regret, and that was something I wanted to fix in my own life, for his sake and for mine.

Also, my mother had died. After she died, performing Winnie became a little less fun. Fun itself became less fun. The performer in me is at its core born of the child who would caper and make rhymes, songs, and dances to get laughs out of Mom and Dad. For two decades Mom was the Kinsey Sicks' biggest fan, even courteously waiting until the day *after* our sold-out 20th Anniversary show before closing her eyes for the last time. In some cultures, mourners tear their clothes or shave their heads. I shed Winnie.

In some ways the trajectory of my life was fixed and foreseeable by the time I was in third grade. A couple pivotal things happened around that time. First, I read a story about the boy who would become the ancient sage, Rabbi Hillel. About his nearly freezing to death on a rooftop eavesdropping on the rabbis discussing Torah. It made me want to risk everything to learn, and it made me decide at age 8 to become a rabbi. The other pivotal thing that year was discovering how easy it was for me to walk in my mother's pumps.

My fate was sealed, yet things didn't play out in expected ways. Years later, when my peers were applying to rabbinical school, I had just come out of the closet. I was in a relationship. No Jewish denomination in 1982 would admit an openly gay student, and it felt deeply wrong to lie to pursue this calling.

Then, within a year, we were in an epidemic centered in my new community. I meandered through some graduate work while being an activist. I shifted to law school to bring a needed skill and credential to my activism. I worked in an ugly fight for gay rights in Chicago. In 1988, exhausted, I moved to San Francisco, just so I could be around lots of queer people. Ultimately, I found my way into a great job at the helm of the AIDS Legal Referral Panel of the San Francisco Bay Area. The Kinsey Sicks started and I met my husband. We formed a family with Anne and Suegee, and when we all moved to Sonoma County together, I found myself, unbidden, on the *bimah* of Congregation Ner Shalom, circling back to a life in the rabbinate.

As Rabbi Akiva, a generation after Hillel, said, "All is foreseen, and yet permission is given." My life as both a rabbi and as a drag queen were both clearly foreseeable. Yet permission was given for me to do it in my own idiosyncratic, meandering, side-door way.

People ask if I miss Winnie. What am I, an idiot? Of course, I miss Winnie. I miss the Kinsey Sicks. I miss the laughing and the rehearsing and the fights. I miss working closely with talented friends who make me laugh. I miss surprising audiences and each other. I even miss the late-night intercity driving, with Jeff Manabat next to me in the passenger seat, faithfully struggling to keep me awake.

With these beloveds, whose eating and sleeping habits I now know much better than I'd like to, I performed everywhere from Montreal to Mykonos, Sydney to St. Petersburg (Florida *and* Russia), not to mention every major US city and a million minor ones that I might never have had the unexpected pleasure to set foot in, from Idaho Falls to Salina, Kansas, to Greenville, SC. We've been Off Broadway, moving to Manhattan just five days before 9/11. We've done Vegas; we've been on the silver screen. We've performed for children, adults, Jews, and Republicans.

I miss who I got to be when I was Winnie. I was, ultimately, not a guy in a dress, and not an attempt at being a woman. I was *me*. I was more *me* on stage in pumps and wig than I have ever been in suit and tie, my body moving with the grace I gained as a third grader, without having to maintain the charade of masculinity that I learned to activate as a child, never particularly successfully. As Winnie, there was a wholeness to me that I miss.

Winnie was a loving friend. Guarded, unguarded, natural. Loyal, lanky, always a-dither. I miss her. She is played by someone else now, much like I played her. She is wonderful, but she is not me, and doesn't need to be. And so it should be. *Winnie est morte, vive la Winnie!*

Minnie's Meringues

I just ate the most wonderful chocolate meringues! They were made by my second cousin Linda, whom I hadn't seen since childhood. I walked into her home in the hills outside Santa Fe, and she greeted me with an overflowing plate of them – marbled cocoa-brown and ivory with crushed nuts punctuating the surface. They were beautiful and delicate. These were the specialty of my grandmother, Minnie Keller, Linda told me. Do I remember?

I didn't remember. I was barely ten when Grandma Minnie died. I remember what she looked like. I remember the buttoned gloves she wore when she went out. Sometimes a whiff of cedar and mothballs brings to mind her little apartment on Estes Avenue in Chicago's East Rogers Park, a block from Touhy Avenue beach. But these meringues? I wasn't certain. Meringues, especially meringues with nuts, are something of an adult taste, and I was a little kid from the suburbs.

I bit in. It dissolved into a rich cocoa puddle on the tongue, and everything in me suddenly said, "Why yes, Grandma Minnie." A few bites later, it was again just a delicious thing. But for that moment, I had the unmistakable sensation of my grandmother next to me, our hearts turned toward each other in a way that hasn't been possible for half a century.

It was spring, and that week was *Shabbat Hagadol*, the Big Shabbos, as it is called, that precedes Pesach. There is something about *Shabbat Hagadol* that stirs together ingredients of both holidays, Sabbath and Passover, honoring the way they both represent remembrance of times past and a peek at the future. Shabbat is a look-back to Creation and a taste of the World to Come. Pesach points back to our escape from slavery, but we close the Seder saying, "Next Year in Jerusalem" – next year in a world of peace. Both Shabbat and Passover Seder conclude with the singing of *Eliyahu Hanavi* – invoking and inviting the presence of our old friend, the prophet Elijah.

Elijah lives in Jewish lore as a kind of mysterious stranger and sometimes-trickster. In Torah, Elijah doesn't die but ascends to heaven in a chariot of flame. *Fwoosh*. Because of this he is rumored to be immortal, now wandering the earth, disguising himself to test people's kindness, to see if now, at last, it is time for a final Redemption. He is rarely seen, but is suspected around every corner, expected at every table.

Elijah loiters particularly around *Shabbat Hagadol*. On this Big Shabbos, we read from the book of Malachi, the last prophet of the Bible, whose name simply means "my angel" and whom some traditions consider to be yet another guise of Elijah, speaking here as God's angel and messenger. The third and final chapter of this short book closes with the prophet Malachi, voicing the words of God, saying, "Behold, I will send you the prophet Elijah before the coming of the great and awesome day of Adonai." This is the source of our tradition that Elijah will be the forerunner of the Messiah. When the world is ready, Elijah will be the one who will lead us, once and for all, from all our narrow places to the great peaceful expanse – expanded consciousness, expanded heart, big wide peace.

Oren and I got a preview of great peaceful expanse just before our arrival in Santa Fe. We had camped overnight in Chaco Canyon, a place we'd visited 21 years earlier, when we were a very new couple. Revisiting this spot was really the whole point of our trip to New Mexico. One thousand years ago, Chaco was the center of a great civilization. The ancients built cities, pueblos, in masonry style – not from brick but from the shale of the mountains themselves, held together with mortar. The ruins of the cities still stand, alongside cliff drawings of spirals, deer, and the ancestors themselves.

On our previous visit, we had an uncanny experience. We were there off season and were the only people visiting. We pitched our tent alongside the stone dwellings, looking out on the vast open canyon. All night long we felt as if we were hearing voices on the wind. Voices of the ancestors – without complete clarity if we were hearing our own ancestors or the ancient pueblo dwellers. Now, two decades later, we hoped to have that experience again, but this time we weren't alone. There was now a visitors' center and other tourists – not a lot, and they were all intrepid and well behaved. Still, as we walked from site to site, we were rarely completely alone, or if we were alone, it was conditional on what or whom we might find around the next bend of the trail.

Chaco was magnificent as ever, but the voices of the ancients were silent. We were no longer in a magical dreamland; we were in a national park. We swallowed our disappointment, being two decades maturer and all. We knew it was a dangerous thing to try to relive an experience of such power. The expectations started high; it was a setup for failure. We crawled into our sleeping bags that night and I imagined sending an angel, the way Jacob did in Torah, to greet the spirits of the ancestors of this place. I imagined it as hard as I could, then fell asleep, awakening intermittently, dreaming of Pesach.

In the morning we got up, warmed ourselves and packed the car. We did one more hike, but the sky looked dark; rain was coming. We went to the visitors' center to send a few postcards and turned around to see that it had started to snow. First it was flurries, then a blizzard. The snow was sticking everywhere. The flakes were huge, as if in this wide wilderness, there was nothing to limit their growth and no advantage to modesty. Yesterday the landscape had been beautiful as expected, but this – this was new, unexpected. Instead of leaving, we drove to one of the ancient pueblos. We walked in the snow, utterly alone, every other tourist having taken cover. The snow, bright white, was riddled through the red-brown Chaco earth, looking like a chocolate meringue, a *Chaco-lit* meringue. It felt in those moments – and who's to say what's real? – like our hearts were turned toward the ancestors and theirs toward us. That in the unexpected snow they had given us the smile we had asked for.

In the Book of Malachi, the Book of My Angel, there is one more final sentence. One last word of prophecy. Not only will Elijah usher in an awesome new era, but "he shall turn the heart of the parents to the children, and the heart of the children to their parents...." What a closing! What a blessing to describe! Not just the earthly relationship of flesh-and-blood people with the generations on either side of them, but a vision of reconciliation and connection with ancestors going back into infinity, and forward for as long as we last. A vision of heart-connection over time. The best and deepest in us, generation after generation, all touching. Ancestors making magic. Descendants imagined into existence. Grandmothers appearing at the taste of chocolate.

Malachi is the traditional text for the Big Shabbos. A Shabbat where we reach back, hand holding hand, to the narrows of Egypt and further back to the very Creation itself. And forward to the expanses that together, in time, we and our loving and skilled descendants can unlock. Each of us is the meeting point of past and future. Each of us a link in that chain. Each plays a small part, or many small parts. And in this sweep of time, we lean forward and back, turning our hearts toward each other. Offering greetings and encouragement across the ages.

There are many ways we do this, big and small. But if you're at a loss and need a more specific instruction, then you can try this:

Take one 6-oz package of semi-sweet chocolate chips and melt them over hot water.

Beat two egg whites with salt until foamy.

Gradually add 1/2 cup of sugar, beating well until stiff points form.

Beat in 1/2 tsp vanilla and 1/2 tsp of vinegar.

Fold in the chocolate and 3/4 cup chopped walnuts.

Drop with a teaspoon onto a greased sheet.

Bake at 350° for ten minutes.

In Heaven's Court

Heaven was abuzz this week. Abuzz in a way that on earth you might perceive as an unusually high incidence of static electricity in the air, or gooseflesh for no reason. In the high reaches, all the angelic beings were on the move: *Malachim* and *cherubim* gathered at fountains and courtyards to wonder together; *seraphim* enfolded themselves in their six wings in disbelief; *ofanim* exchanged meaningful glances with the animal faces of the *chayot*. There was a holy hubbub of curious talk and rarely felt trepidation. How could this be happening? How could Holy Beings oppose the Holy Writ?

It was admittedly a most unusual case. A celestial challenge of divine law. Not a law given to angels who need no law, but a law given to humans. A band of angels suing on behalf of humankind. Trying to upend law given at Sinai. Asking God to eat God's words!

Outrageous. This had never happened before. Not since the Revelation, not since Creation, not since the Singularity that preceded it.

The Archangel Metatron presided over the Heavenly Tribunal. The courtroom was packed. A gavel fell and a crier called out: "*Shema! Shema!* Let all persons having business with the honorable *Yeshivah shel Ma'alah* be admonished to draw near and give their attention, for the Court is now sitting."

The advocates approached the bench. One, clearly human in form, spoke. "Your honors, Rabbi Hillel on behalf of petitioners, the petitioners being a coalition of angels representing the interests of the *Sefirah* of *Chesed* and the steady circulation of love from God into the world and back." Rabbi Hillel had been in happy retirement since his death, spending slow days playing Scrabble with Rabbi Shammai, who always complained that Hillel was making up words. Hillel insisted that if he had a plausible definition, especially a humorous one, his words should count. But now Hillel had been persuaded out of retirement to argue this most unusual case. He stood at the bench and beamed, despite his slightly disheveled appearance, compounded by *matzah* crumbs from the sandwich he'd snuck into the chamber in his pocket.

"And opposing?"

The fiery glow was almost unbearable. "Archangel Gabriel, Solicitor Celestial, Avatar of the *Sefirah* of *Gevurah*, Keeper of Limits and Boundaries, Upholder of the Rule of Law. Your honors."

"Thank you, counselors. Rabbi Hillel, you may begin."

"Your honors, as you know, the present controversy centers around a piece of Torah that begins with the words *kedoshim tihyu ki kadosh ani*. 'Be holy for I am holy.' The specific provisions that follow are considered a Holiness Code. The parties have stipulated that these *mitzvot* are the actions and restrictions humankind was instructed to follow in an attempt to embody holiness."

A nearly imperceptible flutter came over the gallery as the angels present imagined humans, with their seawater bodies and short attention spans, and felt a mixture of amusement, pity, and perhaps resentment. For the blink of an eye, the angelic drone of *holy holy holy* faltered, just a fraction of a second but long enough for the National Geological Survey to record tremors in three distinct points in the Pacific Ocean.

Rabbi Hillel pressed on. "We have no dispute with the first verses of the Holiness Code, your honors. In fact, we applaud the Divine Wisdom that instructs humans to welcome the immigrant, to feed the poor, to respect elders, to observe the Sabbath, to love your neighbor as yourself. We also hold no opinion regarding the puzzling but largely benign prohibitions on planting mixed seeds and wearing linen-wool blends." With this, Rabbi Hillel suddenly became aware of his wrinkled *kapoteh* and moved a hand as if to smooth it before realizing the futility of the effort. "We do not object to any of those laws, your honors. However, where we see a tremendous, if previously overlooked, injustice is—"

"Rabbi," the Chief Justice interrupted, "let us first take up the jurisdictional issue. By what authority does humankind seek to annul a law given by God? Are the earthly courts insufficient to handle the resolution of this matter?"

"Your honors," replied Rabbi Hillel, "we humans are gifted by our Creator with some small intelligence that we bring to difficult questions. We do not claim your wisdom of course; after all, as the Psalm says, just below angels are we. Yet as we humbly ponder the law and the very real lives of flesh and blood – no offense, your honors – to which they must apply, we try to do so in the name of heaven. As it says in Talmud, *eylu v'eylu divrei Elohim chayim*. All of our conflicting points of view as we debate are in fact the living words of God."

"Yes, Rabbi" interrupted Chief Justice Metatron, "you are doing heaven's work; it has been delegated to humankind to do. So why bother us? Why do you humans not just do it?"

"Yes, your honor. We could; we would; we do. But there is precedent for a more direct exchange between heaven and earth in certain legal matters, for instance, when there is imminent danger to God's creation – or even to God's reputation. In such cases, petitions have gone directly to heaven. For instance, Father Abraham bargaining for the lives of the people of Sodom."

"It did him no good," spat Gabriel.

"His intervention was permitted even if his goal was not achieved," replied the sage. "And at times, in our toughest of cases, heaven has, unbidden, sent a *bat kol* – a prophetic voice – to guide us."

"Which guidance you have always ignored," countered the archangel.

"In any event, I remind the Court that I am not here representing humankind but rather an intervening angelic body. The Coalition of Heavenly Entities Supporting Equality in Desire. C.H.E.S.E.D." Rabbi Hillel glanced at the gallery where his clients waved a rainbow – a real rainbow in this case. He looked back at the panel. "These are angels who, observing the human struggle over the law we will discuss, are moved to bring about its nullification."

"Your honor," broke in the Archangel. "These C.H.E.S.E.D. people cannot decide to challenge the law. They are angels. They have no free will. They are limbs of the Divine. They respond only to Divine Thought."

"And yet," Hillel replied, "here we are. They are certainly responding to some element of the Divine Will, as are you, Counselor. We are aware of many aspects of the Divine – Truth, Beauty, Majesty, Mercy. Maybe it is time we add one: Ambivalence."

There was a collective gasp in the courtroom at the Rabbi's *chutzpah*, and this time the low monotone of *holy holy holy* broke off entirely. On earth, souffles fell and many thousands of individual socks instantly vanished unobserved from electric dryers.

"Rabbi Hillel will please leave the nature of the Divine to us," scolded the Chief Justice. "In the meantime, please move on to the merits of your petition."

"Thank you, your honors. *Yeshivah shel Ma'lah*, Judges most High, we are here today to correct a wrong. We are here to overturn Verse 13 of Chapter 20 of the third book of Torah, which says, "Man shall not lie with man as with a woman; it is an abomination; they shall be put to death." But I wish to begin with another text altogether. *Shir Hashirim*, Song of Songs, our people's greatest love poetry. "Let him kiss me with the kisses of his mouth, for your love is better than wine."

"Relevance!" barked Gabriel.

"His left hand is under my head; his right hand embraces me."

"Your Honor!"

"Justices, my successor in life and colleague in Paradise, the great Rabbi Akiva ben Yosef, noted that Song of Songs is a holy book. Is this disputed?"

"No objection," said Gabriel cautiously.

"Rabbi Akiva also said that while all the writings of our Writ are holy, *Shir Hashirim* is the *Kodesh Kodashim* – the Holy of Holies – and that the whole world is not worth the day that *Shir Hashirim* was created. He says this because while the other books give important laws and tell important stories, only *Shir Hashirim* comes close to describing the love of God for Creation, and the love of Creation for God. Human love, human longing is an earthly embodiment of this love; it is the most deeply felt way for our very limited kind to experience the Great Holiness. And so human love, human longing, in all its forms, is holy."

"What?" cried Gabriel. "Surely you are not suggesting that what Leviticus makes abomination, Song of Songs makes holy? To claim that the right to engage in such conduct is implicit in the concept of holiness is, at best, facetious."

The angels in the C.H.E.S.E.D. section began to boo, but in a loving way.

"Yes, Rabbi," probed the Chief Justice, "what are the parameters of your position? Are you saying all human sex is holy?"

"No, your Honor. Only sex that is steeped in love. Only sex approached with an open heart. Oh, and sex that is really, really fun."

"Rabbi, the Holiness Code also prohibits sex with slaves, sex with close family members, sex that is adulterous, sex with animals. Are you proposing those prohibitions be lifted as well?"

"Those prohibitions are distinguishable, your honor. They address relationships with inherent power disparities, relationships where the parties do not have equal ability to say 'yes' or 'no' – or even any ability. And the adultery prohibition reflects an awareness that there are others who might be hurt by such a relationship. But the provision we challenge today, Leviticus 20:13, has no mention of power disparity, not a hint of exploitation. It applies to consenting adults, yet their holy act of love is punishable by death."

"Your honor," chimed in the Solicitor Celestial, "other laws in the Holiness Code that exact a death penalty have simply been ignored by humankind or commuted to another type of punishment. A child cursing its parents, for example. I can't remember the last time I saw one of them stoned – well, you know what I mean. In any event, I know it is unlike me to say so, but flexibility has been demonstrated in the application of the laws of Leviticus. Humankind takes many of these rules with a grain of salt."

"And yet," responded the sage, plucking some stray horseradish from his beard and absentmindedly removing it to his tongue, "in the case of this particular prohibition, humankind is uncharacteristically literal. The law is still taken at face value in many cultures and many places on earth, and in some of them still invokes a death penalty. In other places the death penalty takes the form of violence in the streets or the suicide of young people. No, your honors, as for taking this abomination thing with a grain of salt, it seems much of humanity is on a salt-free diet. Ah, wait, I misspeak," continued Hillel. "One flexibility is commonly granted: women who lie with women, not mentioned in the law at all, are, thanks to Leviticus, treated to the same condemnation in much of human society. Living in the shadow of this prohibition is a source of profound sadness. Since Sinai, humans have been pressured into marriages without love, from which many more people suffer. Humans have been riddled with shame and self-judgment. This law has brought on a world of suffering."

"But your honors," thundered Archangel Gabriel, "even if this is so, it is for humans to work out. Let them make change however they go about making change. I don't understand what the rabbi here expects us to do about it. Shouldn't this unfold in a human way, country by country, society by society?"

"Your honors," answered Rabbi Hillel, "I submit to you that Leviticus 20:13 was not correct when it was given at Sinai, and it is not correct today. It ought not to remain binding precedent and should be overruled."

In the gallery you could hear a pin drop, and many dancing angels falling right off the head of it. Rabbi Hillel lifted his hands in supplication. "It is not for our sake that I ask this, your honors, but for yours. Words of Torah should give honor to God. This law has caused good and holy people to dismiss you, and God, and Torah itself, from their lives. They have come to trust the holiness of their love; they just think that You don't. There is imminent threat to God's reputation here. It is not for the sake of the people currently called "gay" that we seek redress. Because they will continue on and fight their fight, along with their friends and families and allies, and they will keep loving each other despite. They will make art and song about their struggles and jokes to make light of the indignity of it. They will change the world, with or without you. It is not for them but for heaven that this correction must be made."

"But Rabbi," said Metatron, the Chief Justice, sounding now old and tired himself, "what can we do at this point? This has gone on so long."

Rabbi Hillel thought at this moment that something passed between himself and the Chief Justice. The Chief Justice, who was the only angel in the spheres who was once a man, Chanoch, a particular beloved of God, who could not bear him to die and installed him instead in the heavenly court, alive and immortal. The Chief

Justice must be able to remember back to his earthly existence, his love, his longing, his long walks with God. The Chief Justice would help. The Chief Justice would cast his vote for *Chesed*.

"Rabbi," the Chief Justice called Hillel back to attention. "Torah has already been given. What relief can we offer?"

Hillel held Metatron's eye as he delivered his unorthodox request. "Your honor, in the rabbinic academies, we have a phrase that guides us: *Eyn mukdam um'uchar batorah*. There is no 'before' or 'after' in Torah. Time itself is not irrevocable. So we implore you: erase this error now so that it will not even exist at Sinai. Undo it now so that it will never have been. Let the world unfold without it. Let love prosper. Let this particular hatred and shame never get born. See how a more loving world fares. See how–"

A flame came down from the sky to rest on an altar next to the Chief Justice. Rabbi Hillel sighed. "I see I have used my time."

For a moment, the eyes of Metatron, the once-human Chief Justice, seemed lost in thought.

"Rabbi, a question from upstairs. If there is no 'before' or 'after,' why should we act now?"

"Because, your honor, if not now, when?"

The Chief Justice seemed about to say something but changed his mind. "Thank you, Counsel," he remarked at last. "The case is submitted."

The *Go'el* of *Boulevard de Sébastopol*

It was late Saturday night – well past midnight – when I walked home up Boulevard de Sébastopol in Paris. I was alone, and that itself was a quirky fact. It was a family vacation for our two children, 12 and 8, and we four adults who raised them. We had been invited to spend a week with friends in a farmhouse in the south. When we said our goodbyes there, we headed north to the City of Light.

We had arranged an Air B&B, but when we arrived, we found the apartment full of dust and mold. After a little cleaning it would work for the two hearty children and two hearty adults. But one of our co-parents, with severe asthma, could not sit for an hour in the apartment, let alone sleep there. So our co-parents went off in search of a hotel room that was allergen-free, and Oren and I settled in with the kids. The apartment was dark and laid out awkwardly. It was hot, and street noise blared into the open windows, but it was good enough. For the next couple days we'd return from our sightseeing exhausted anyway. A quick snack, and we'd surely fall sound asleep to the ambient sounds of motorcycles and quarreling lovers.

We had planned to exploit the perks of having the children so outnumbered. Each couple would be afforded a night out on the town, while the other couple minded the kids. However, once our co-parents were installed in a hotel room across town, that plan dissolved. Oren saw my disappointment, so he suggested I go out alone – sightsee, carouse – and he would do so on another night. And so I did. Even though it was late by the time we settled the kids into bed, I went out and made a good show of having some fun, my tourist map of gay Paris held tight in my fist. But it wasn't the same without him. It felt more duty than spree. So at a very respectable 1:00 am I headed north toward our little apartment on the edge of *le Marais*, an ancient neighborhood once home to nobility, now shared by longstanding Jews and gentrifying gays. I considered walking up Rue St. Martin or Rue St. Denis, but I'd already walked on both of those that day, and I preferred the road less traveled.

The businesses lining Boulevard de Sébastopol were closed; their aluminum shutters pulled down to the sidewalk and locked. I was alone on the shadowed sidewalk, at least for a block or so ahead and behind. This was, however, an important northbound artery from the center of Paris. Cars sped past me on the three-lane, one-way street, their red taillights peppering my vision. As I walked, something in the air – nighttime urban smells maybe – brought me suddenly to my great grandmother's apartment on Chicago's lakeshore. My father, a bandleader, would typically have a gig somewhere downtown on Friday nights, but my mother's parents, aunts and uncles would all gather at the matriarch's home for dinner and conversation. Instead of sitting in the house alone with us those nights, Mom would gather us up and bring us to her 90-year-old grandmother's. The Shabbat candles would be lit. I would drink Fresca, which we never had at home. Sometimes, if we were there late enough, my father would show up after his gig, still in a tuxedo, and my great aunts would fuss over him and make him a late plate of dinner.

This memory, uninvited, had not come to me in many, many years. I walked up Boulevard de Sébastopol with my mind 6000 miles and 45 years away. I was jolted back to myself by car horns. The traffic passing on my left seemed to hesitate for a moment. And here perceptions began to change, because things happened quicker than I could make sense of them. People were laying on the horn. A car just ahead was driving the wrong way down the one-way street.

I was mid-block, on the sidewalk, the street on my left, an unlit, empty park on the right. The car facing the wrong way spun into the alley just ahead of me, slammed on the brakes and stopped in the crosswalk, blocking my path. Four large men screamed at me out the open car windows – perhaps in French, perhaps another language. I stopped, uncomprehending, as they threw open the car doors, poured out and began to run toward me. In the hand of one of them was a gun, with a towel wrapped around the grip and the hand holding it; the long barrel in the air briefly, then pointed at me.

This is the point at which very fast calculation happened. Looking at their size, their distance, their speed. I remembered a Queer Nation self-defense class I took in the early 1990s, when gay-bashings were frequent in San Francisco. I remembered Liz, our instructor, telling us that if someone tries to get you into a car, you must fight, because what will happen in the car or at the destination is far worse than what will happen in the struggle to get free. All these things registered with lightning speed in my cerebral cortex. Or maybe my amygdala short-circuited the entire cognitive operation. Or maybe – and now that this idea has occurred to me, it is the only way I can remember it – a voice spoke softly and firmly into my ear: *run*.

I about-faced and took off. Probably 25 years older than my pursuers, I realized I could not outrun them if they were intent on catching me. In the swirl of thoughts, I wondered if this was a game or a dare, or if they thought I was someone else, or if it was just that I was a lone gay man or a lone Jew or a lone human at just the moment that they had settled on the idea of a night of terror. I knew that if they got me, I would be dead, or my life changed forever – my husband and our family's vacation cut short; their lives marked; perhaps not ever knowing what happened to me. I thought of them, I thought of my mother. I anticipated all their heartbreak, and it broke my heart.

In a flash I knew what I needed to do: run into traffic. Cars were still speeding past, their headlights now in front of me, but I determined I had a better chance of surviving being hit by a car than of surviving these men. So, with a sensation almost of being guided by hands on my shoulders, I dove into the roadway, yelling and waving my arms. Somehow, the glare of headlights became a field of protective light between me and the oncoming cars. I made it across to the other side, now only one pursuer behind me: the one with the gun.

I ran and quickly realized that this side of the street was even darker and emptier than where I'd come from. I now saw some pedestrians across the street and again I dove into the river of traffic, swimming upstream into speeding headlights. And again, a way parted for me, and I reached the far shore. This time my assailant reconsidered. He stood on the other side of the street looking at me, and then turned back.

I saw their car pull away. I tried to alert people on the street, but with my frayed nerves and broken French, I certainly seemed a madman. I was afraid of what the young men might go on to do, but I was also afraid to stay on the street to look for police – *what if they circle around and come back?* I felt helpless to even explain. All I wanted was to be back inside with my husband and kids, with this now-dangerous city on the other side of a locked door. Hyperalert, overstimulated, bewildered that once again the street was behaving as if it were just a place, I got myself back to the apartment. I woke Oren and told him what happened. Finally, I curled up with our sleeping 8-year-old and held him tight.

I rarely speak about this experience. I told a couple friends when I got home but I didn't want my mother ever to have to picture me being chased by gunmen. I never wrote or sermonized about it, as I might have with other challenging experiences. I also held back because of the awareness that I had escaped while other people have not. What are the storytelling rights of a close call, a narrow escape, by someone for whom violence is an anomaly? And once you opt not to tell it, what effect does that have? For me, as a secret, the Paris experience became weighted with shame. Being a queer out on the street, alone at night, what else did I expect?

Nietzsche says, "what doesn't kill you makes you stronger," which is obviously untrue. What doesn't kill you leaves you guilty, scarred, marked. It took years to return to this experience and to the voice at my ear – a voice that was present in my remembering but not clearly in my experience in the moment. Had some kind of *hashgachah pratit* – a personal providence – guided me through that moment? An angelic intervention, hands on my shoulders? Because even now, I can feel those hands.

In the subsequent years, something always surged upward in me whenever, in the course of Torah readings, we reached the end of the Book of Genesis where Jacob, on his deathbed, offers a blessing to his grandsons, Ephraim and Menasseh. He says something curious: *hamalach hago'el oti mikol ra y'varech et han'arim* – "May the angel who saves me from all harm bless these boys..." It is not clear what angel Jacob is referring to as he looks back on his life. His history of divine interaction is abundant but zigzaggy, involving angels and dreams more often than direct prophecy. Now, at the end of his life, he blesses his grandsons by invoking a redeeming angel that we have never heard of before. Who or what is this angel?

Rashi understands the *malach hago'el* – the Redeeming Angel – to be an individual angel that was routinely sent to Jacob in his most challenging moments. Other medieval commentators see the *malach hago'el* as either an epithet for God or as God wearing the thinnest of veils. The Hebrew of the full passage supports this reading; the grammar wants it. Ultimately, Jacob *feels* himself to have been protected, and that is the important piece. That protection, though sourced in God, came in a form that he experienced as personal and human in scale. Help that came directly from a God larger than the Universe would have felt impersonal, even random.

I remember that dark night in Paris. My heart, my bones, my spirit, do not want what happened to be random. I don't want my survival to have been odds or luck. I want to feel that in that direst of moments, the extra support I received was somehow personal: the guiding hands on my shoulders, the voice speaking at my ear, the wash of light buffering me from speeding boxes of metal and glass.

Maybe it wasn't angelic. Maybe my flight response worked so quickly that my body acted before my thought could catch up, creating a sense of disembodiment and dislocation. Was it my amygdala whispering in my ear? Or was it guidance from the ancestors? After all, I had just been thinking about them moments before. Had I summoned them and had they lent their protective influence to my rescue? Or maybe it's something else. Maybe we all live in multiple realms – a physical one in which we are all separate, and a spiritual realm in which we are connected with each other and with the mystery. Maybe I drew on the wisdom and instinct of the version of myself that is higher, deeper, more connected with the transcendent. I was my own angel, my own angelic self, and the press on my shoulders was, in this sense, the weight of my own wings.

All those things are possible! But I confess I have settled into remembering that night not only as one of danger but as one of angelic protection. I don't know if the intervention was executed by a personal *malach go'el*, or if this was the Go'el of *Blvd de Sébastopol* guarding the clueless stranger blundering through its realm. But whoever, whatever, that angelic presence was, we have now touched, and I recognize its feel in my memory.

Now in my bedtime *shema*, I often think of our two boys, now adults in the world, but asleep that night in Paris, and I feel guiding hands on my shoulders. I say, *Hamalach hago'el oti mikol ra y'varech et han'arim* – may the angel who protects me from harm bless these boys, and all who come after.

Reverse 23

I have always lived in your house
with blessing and kindness at my back.
What an overflowing cup of blessing —
luxurious as oil poured on my brow.
Even my troubles join me at the table
for this banquet of life!
I am comforted leaning on you,
who soothes my fear in shadowed valleys
and guides me on paths of righteousness.
My spirit is renewed.

Here, at the waters of rest,
on the bed of fresh grasses,
nothing is missing,
Shepherd of mine.

A Ghost of *Shtetl* Future

I took a walk not long ago – not here in hilly Sonoma County, but in one of my family's ancestral *shtetlech*. A town called Krynki in Polish; the Jews called it Krinek. It is next to the Belarus border, not far from Bialystok, in what was once Grodno Gubernya. My ancestors lived there and also kept a tiny farm in the neighboring village of Kolonja Izaaka.

I walked there on a Sunday afternoon, again the next day at bedtime, and a few more times over the week. I first visited Krinek in 2007 with my mother and sister, and we strolled there two consecutive March days, one sunny and one full of dark, regretful rain. This time, I had two beautiful sunny days which were, in fact, the same beautiful sunny day, because I wasn't there in the flesh. My visit was virtual, and I was a kind of cyber-ghost.

I have always been drawn to the places of our collective Jewish past and prone to getting stuck in the places of my family's specific past. My iPhone clock tells me the time in Bialystok and the weather app lets me know when it's snowing in Vilna. Sometimes, I want an aerial view, and I hurtle myself aloft with satellite images on Google Earth.

Today, that was what I'd intended to do: a little look-down, or look-over, of Krinek. In the process, I saw that Google Streetview was now available for Poland. Since the time of my physical visit, some driver hired by Google had driven every street of Krinek with a 360-degree multi-directional camera on the roof, operating with sensors and a rolling shutter. The camera caught imagery from all directions – forward, backward, sides, up and down, the camera's gaze waving like a *lulav*. Then the massive Google brain stitched these shots together to create an immersive and navigable photo that includes every street, every highway, every publicly accessible house in the village – and everywhere else in the world that Google drivers have penetrated. While most people use this function in mundane ways, like seeing what the restaurant looks like that they're trying to find, I visit the *shtetl*.

In my experience, most American Jews were not bequeathed a meaningful memory of the Old Country. Some might know the country or region, but few can name a town. A couple generations before me, the town continued to be a marker of identity, even in America. The immigrant generations belonged to fraternal organizations, *landsmanshaftn*, organized to help others from their own *shtetl*. My great-grandparents were linchpins in Chicago's *Krinker Verein*, the organization for immigrants from Krinek. My great-grandfather headed the *Chevra Kadisha*, the Burial Society. The members of the *Verein* bought and walled off a section of Chicago's monumental Waldheim Cemetery, so that people born within a mile of each other on the other side of the planet could be buried within feet of each other here.

The generations of Jews who could freely talk about their ancestral towns and villages are gone, but I like to be an aberration in my generation. Sometimes it's meaningless. Flashing my Krinek credentials never got me a conversation with Studs Terkel, whose parents are buried next to my great-grandparents. But occasionally I meet someone else like me, like the owner of a local coffee company giving out samples at our grocery. Our young teenager was with me and hungrily spied the sugar cubes on the sampling table. He joked I should put a cube between my teeth, like my great-grandfather did. I was pleased he'd remembered that story, and I reminded him that he did that not with coffee but with a *glezl tey* – a glass of tea. The coffee entrepreneur looked up and said, "He was Russian?" I said, "Well, between Bialystok and Grodno." To my delight, he said, "My family comes from a *shtetl* between Bialystok and Grodno too." It wasn't the same one, but nearby, and suddenly we were neighbors. *Landsmen*, as we say in Yiddish. So I started buying their coffee because isn't that the job of *landsmen*, to help each other get a leg up in this golden land of opportunity?

So here I am, back in Krinek, with the help of Google Streetview. I move about the village, navigating with the touchpad of my laptop. Forward, right, stop. Turn around. Look at the houses in all directions. I can transport myself any direction at will, as long as I don't try to go where the Google car couldn't reach. I feel like a ghost, bound by the kind of arbitrary rules that bind ghosts in every legend and horror film. I can go toward the houses, but I can't go in. I can float down a street but not a footpath or a blind alley. I am invisible. I can't go in the water. I am stuck in the same day all the time. My sight is impaired: there are places that are distorted, pixelated; houses sometimes bend or bulge on the periphery.

Being a ghost here seems fitting. This was a town that in its heyday had a population of 4000; 80% of them were Jews. There were synagogues, a *mikveh*, a *yeshivah*. It was a town of labor unrest, where striking tannery workers managed to win a more humane workday of a mere twelve hours. There were reprisals by the Russian Army against the town's Jews for leading those strikes, beginning around 1902, prompting masses of Krinkers to leave for North and South America — my ancestors among them.

There are no more Jews in Krinek – not a single one, as far as I know. In 1941 they were corralled into a long, narrow ghetto running along the river from the town center to Gabarska Street, where the Jewish tanneries stood. A year later the Jews were gone altogether and Krynki became a ghost town.

How does one live in a ghost town? I don't know. The 800 Christian Poles who remained somehow managed it. They spent the Communist Era and beyond slowly occupying the empty space. It took 65 years for the population count to return to 4000, 65 years of pushing back the ghost town street by street, house by house. My mind gets stuck on what this process looked like. I can't help but think that for every one of those houses, there was a moment when someone pried a *mezuzah* off a doorpost. Maybe they did it filled with grief, maybe full of gloat, but it was a real thing, both physical and symbolic, that happened at each of those houses.

Roaming the streets of Krynki, invisible, propelled not by legs on pavement but by fingers on a keyboard thousands of miles away, I look at those houses, at the unevenness of the paint on the doorposts revealing where *mezuzot* had once, and for generations, been affixed. The town still feels empty, and though I call it a ghost town, I am the only ghost there. The Bashevis Singer-style phantoms you would expect decamped half a century ago, boarding ships to who knows where.

Still, my odd, ghostly presence allows me to see somehow between the pixels and perceive that the celestial beings have not quite given up on this broken place. At each doorpost I see an angelic trio, right out of Isaiah, their upper wings enfolding their heads like turbans or scarves, their lower wings wrapping their bodies like a gabardine, their middle wings draping over their shoulders like a *tallit*. They look like Jews, they look like my grandparents, but on second thought, they don't look human at all. They look like all people and all creatures. They are all genders and their eyes are aflame. They are *seraphim* - fiery angels, determined to burn off the pain, the trauma of the past.

They face the indentation in the paint where the *mezuzah* once hung, the place of the crowbar. I can see them clearly, even while the house itself is blurred and the street buckled from too many camera angles. They face the *mezuzah*, rocking on their toes, chanting *kadosh kadosh kadosh*. "Holy! Holy! Holy!" They go about their work unfazed by people coming and going out of those doors. Their voices are exciting the atoms, animating the molecules. A kind of light, not quite light as we know it, pools on the doorpost in the shape of a *mezuzah*. The angels are healing the house.

I do not know to what end the angels' project was undertaken. Is the healing for the sake of the Jews who were lost? Or for the Polish children living, unaware, in the house? Or for God's own sake – God, whose hands are voluntarily tied and kept from tampering with history, and who desires our forgiveness for this questionable decision?

Whatever its cosmic purpose, I was suddenly able to see what the angels were aiming at. They were crafting a version of Krinek that could live in *Olam Haba*, the World to Come. Now I could see it, flickering before me. A glowing Shabbos *shtetl*, a hubbub of light under a starry Chagall sky.

A vision of brokenness healed, life reanimated, filled my mind and warmed my blood like fiery plum brandy. I breathed in the familiar Polish air, catching a hint of pine trees, candlewax, and warm *challah*. It was now Shabbos in the village. The sounds of wordless Chasidic melodies drifted out of one nearby window, revolutionary anthems out of another. I close my eyes. A whisper of *kadosh kadosh kadosh* emerges from my lips as I close my laptop.

Joseph's Bones

It's a cold Shabbat morning in December and I am sitting vigil at the deathbed of Joseph. I am not alone but surrounded by members of the Taproot Community who have gathered this week in Bolinas, California – Coast Miwok land, on the ocean, in the mist, atop the Pacific Plate, on the other side of the world from Joseph's *Mitzrayim*. We are bundled in jackets and blankets, each of us seared on one side by heat lamps like uneven toast. We sit on straw mats in a large, open tent.

The Torah scroll is also down low, close to the Earth. We have a folding table – still folded – lying flat on a Persian rug. The tabletop is wrapped in fancy cloth and the Torah scroll relaxes gently upon it, draped by an oversized, ocean-blue *tallit*. Members of the cohort have been leading the morning prayer, and we are now approaching the Torah service and the close of the Book of Genesis.

My friend and teacher, Rabbi Diane Elliot, opens the Torah to offer the first reading. When we chanted this same *parashah* at the Taproot Gathering three years ago, she effected a tremendous *tikkun* by chanting Dinah back into the blessings Jacob offered his sons. This year, she is reading about the burial of Jacob in the Cave of Machpelah. She shares a *midrash* that on the journey to Canaan with Jacob's body, the caravan passed by the pit into which Joseph had, as a youth, been cast by his brothers. Rabbi Diane expounds on the necessity of returning to the places of our trauma for healing to happen. She chants the Hebrew, and our hearts open to the insistent and ancient pain we all carry. When she finishes, we breathe, and several members of the group chant the next verses of Torah.

Then it is my turn to complete Joseph's story. I have been in relationship with Joseph for years – wondering, puzzling, collecting the many hints in Torah that point to some queerness, some difference in Joseph's gender. Oddities in the text that gravitate around Joseph's looks, clothing, emotions, body, and social role. His womb that is awakened upon seeing his younger brother Benjamin. His knees that are referenced in connection to birth, in ways otherwise reserved for women of Torah. This has all been churning in my head for years, and a couple weeks earlier I had even posted a lengthy essay about it on my blog, but I had never chanted any of Joseph's story from Torah itself. And now I am to chant his death.

I approach the scroll and share some of the things I've observed about Joseph. I preview the reading, foreshadowing the verse that tells us that the elderly Joseph's great-grandchildren were born on Joseph's knees – a seeming reference to a birthing posture in which a laboring mother braces against the knees of a more senior woman. I explain how I see Joseph at the end of his life – no, at the end of *their* life – at last being fully at home in their gender, a gender that permits them to be in the birthing chamber with the women. This, just a chapter after the dying Jacob belatedly offers his child Joseph "the blessings of breast and womb."

The Taproot members are the right group for this Torah. They are cultural healers and spiritual activists, queer or allies, most of them younger than I am by at least a quarter century. Some of them identify and live as non-binary and use they/them pronouns in their daily life – a choice I too might have made if the option were available to me when I was younger. But I feel too old and creaky for that change now, no matter how well it would suit me. I continue to wear my he/him pronouns like a frumpy, ill-fitting cardigan.

As I speak, my eyes wander down to Joseph's final words in

Torah. Joseph offers a prophecy that God will one day remember the Children of Israel and bring them out of Egypt. When that happens, Joseph demands, *v'ha'alitem et atzmotai mizeh*, "raise up my bones from here." I had never fully noticed that it doesn't say, "carry my bones to the land of Canaan," which would have limited its meaning to the geographic. Instead, Joseph says, "raise up my bones," without a specific destination identified in that verse.

The word for "bone" – *etzem* – has metaphoric meaning in Hebrew. It is not only the body's physical frame, but one's essence, substance, or even self. Joseph's command can be read as metaphorical: "lift up my selves." Suddenly, and for the first time, I hear Joseph asking the Children of Israel – asking us – to raise up, to honor, to carry forward with us, Joseph's complex and multiple qualities. Their fullness. Their *selves*.

That is what we are about to do, even if it has taken 4000 years and 7000 miles to make good on the promise. The group makes the Torah blessing. I chant the melodies I'd practiced – *mah'pach, pashta, katon*. In my necktie and multi-colored Shabbat skirt, my pulse begins racing. I see how my whole life has led to this moment: my gender journey, my Jewish learning, my queer family, my wounds, my joys, my drag. All of it: preparation.

I reach the phrase about great-grandchildren being born on Joseph's knees and I slap my own knees so that we are all together in that anticipated moment. When I reach the last verse, the verse in which Joseph dies, I invite the group to come closer, and they do. We are all on our knees, a tight circle surrounding the Torah as if at Joseph's deathbed. We are Joseph's family, the grandchildren birthed on Joseph's knees. We are standing vigil at the bedside. I grip the Torah rollers and suddenly they are Joseph's hands in mine.

My eyes close as blessing begins to pour out, that we might all be seen in our complexity. That all our bones, our substance, our selves, should be uplifted. That we should feel no part of us to be less worthy. That we might see every bit of ourselves and each other as *tzelem Elohim* – the image of the Divine. I feel tears welling up and hear the quiet weeping of others around me – weeping at the death of Joseph, or maybe weeping from the grief of realizing how many parts of ourselves we have considered beneath blessing.

Silence falls. We sit, stunned, as one does after attending a death. Out of the silence comes the voice of one Taprooter, chanting a healing prayer, and we begin singing for Joseph's healing and for our own. We have all been called to be here in this moment. To witness. To bless. To cry. To heal. Our prayers and blessings pour into Torah, back to Joseph, and we feel blessings pouring forward to us.

We have raised up Joseph's bones this day, Joseph's selves. We have raised them right out of the scroll and into our hearts and hands, right into the bright winter daylight of Bolinas, California. *Chazak chazak v'nit'chazek*, we say – the traditional words when completing a book of Torah. "Be strong, be strong, let us strengthen each other." We dry our eyes, tuck some of Joseph's sparkling and intricate selves into the pockets of our souls, and look at one another again – aglow, open, knowing.

Such Stuff as Dreams are Made Of

The dream came while I was performing with the Kinsey Sicks in Puerto Vallarta, Mexico. It was hot and I went to sleep with balcony doors open, overlooking the dazzling blue Bay of Banderas. It was just a month after my mother's death; in fact, it was my first day out of *shloshim*, the traditional 30-day mourning period.

In my dream, I walked into a *fin-de-siecle* European sanitorium. A balding, bespectacled doctor was there with my mother. He had figured out what was wrong with her brain and it was an easy fix. He'd just gone ahead and done it and she was instantly okay – younger and stronger than I'd ever seen her, luminous really, and he said there was no longer a reason for her to be there. So I took her in the car and we sped through towns and forests until we were driving up a mountain rising out of the Aegean Sea – climbing, climbing as if up to Olympus itself, Mediterranean blue as far as the eye could see.

We drove, sitting side by side in the car, just as we had been at the moment of her stroke. At this point my waking memory began to seep in. I realized something was not right. I pulled over and told her that we'd already sat *shivah* for her, and it had been so sad. I fell on her shoulder, and she held me while I cried.

That's pretty much the entirety of the dream. It was beautiful and sad, and not particularly mysterious. I was venting my grief, letting go of the weeks – and years – of worry about her health and safety. My subconscious giving me a chance to feel some peace. But the thing is, it didn't just feel like my subconscious or like my imagination. It felt messagey, like I know grieving people sometimes experience. It felt like a hello. A message from Mom that she was okay, her suffering healed. And its feeling that way was, for me, a problem, because I am, in part, a skeptic. Despite my seeking and my storytelling of connections between worlds and my unending references to angels, I inevitably hold some amount of it within quotation marks.

Sometimes I soar aloft but then, thud, I land back in my flightless day-to-day. Maybe this comes from my mother's Litvak background. The visiting Litvak, or Lithuanian Jew, always plays the role of the doubter in Chasidic tales, scoffing at the rebbe's wonders, until he is won over in the end.

Some skepticism is grounded right in our ancient texts. While Talmud tells us that an uninterpreted dream is like a letter left unread, it goes on to say that our dreams are only $1/60^{th}$-part prophecy. "Don't count on your dreams for guidance," imply the rabbis of antiquity. "The prophecy in them is negligible." But tantalizingly, negligible is not the same as non-existent. One-sixtieth is tiny but quantifiable. It's one minute of every hour you sleep. That's 6, 7, 8 minutes of prophecy a night, which really isn't so bad. But frustratingly, Talmud gives no guidance as to how to identify which eight minutes are gold.

So I dance the dance of paradox. I long for mystical experience, for conversation with God and angels, and visits to non-corporeal realms. I am also quick to pooh-pooh the woo-woo. When I experience something transcendent, my next instinct is to douse the experience in a bucket of cold water. But there are times when the mystical is too pressing, too inexplicable. Which brings me back to this dream.

I woke up and looked out at the blue Mexican water, feeling sad and feeling spoken to. I couldn't shake the sense that she had just been there, holding me. I posted the dream on Facebook, asking, "How can we ever tell what is a message and what is our imagining?" Instantly people began weighing in. They all said, "Of course it's a message," causing me to slam my laptop shut, muttering, "How would *you* know?"

I got up, dressed, and walked to the *mercado* for fruit and vegetables. On my way back, I wandered through the old town, wondering how one can ever tell if such an experience is anything more than the heart's wishful thinking, the brain concocting medicine for a spirit in need of it? I posed the "how can you ever know for sure" question in my head as clearly as one might pose an inquiry to a Magic-8 Ball. If only one could see a sign of some sort! Just as this request for a sign formed on my lips, I looked up and saw one. I was standing in front of Club Mañana, a former dance club and theater where the Kinsey Sicks had performed for several seasons. *Mañana* was now for sale, and I was staring at the *En Venta* – the "For Sale" sign. My eyes were drawn down to the large-lettered name of the realtor.

Marilyn Newman.

My mother's maiden name.

If I'd seen it in a movie, I would have snickered at its heavy-handedness, but in real life I stood there, feeling stupid. That because of my insistent grinchiness, a hello from my mother had to come endorsed with a signature before I could believe it. Was this a coincidence? Of course it was. Might I have noticed this *gringa* realtor's name, this *ersatz* Marilyn Newman, on some other "For Sale" sign in Puerto Vallarta a year or two earlier? I might have noticed it and called my mother on the phone to say, "You'll never guess what I saw today!" I might have, but I didn't. I only saw it in the slightly altered consciousness that followed the dream.

Rebbe Nachman of Bratzlav taught that every blade of grass has a song of its own, a melody that comes from the sweetness of the water and the setting of the pasture. The song of the grass informs the song of the sheep that eat it, and the song of the shepherd who spends days lying on it, watching the sheep. Every living thing – no, every *thing* – has a kind of music that we can hear if we open to it.

Meanwhile, Talmud teaches us that no blade of grass grows without an angel standing there, encouraging it, saying, "Grow! Grow!"

These two teachings combine to describe a universe full of aliveness, in which on some level everything is talking to everything. The Divine talks and Creation talks back, in a great, gorgeous cacophony not dissimilar to a Jewish dinner table. If we are in the right state of consciousness, we might hear some of the crosstalk that we otherwise would never tune into – the crosstalk that sometimes seems to respond to a question in our hearts, or calls us to action when we need it, or calls us to attention at just the right moment.

Sometimes the crosstalk of the Universe comes to us in the language of coincidence because it is abundant and we all understand its grammar. Coincidence is the Esperanto of Divine communication. At least that's my experience. For others it might be quiet insight, and who knows, maybe others hear voices. But coincidence, synchronicity, in my experience, is always worth pausing to notice.

Or maybe there is no call from the divine. Maybe there is no prophecy in dreams. Maybe coincidence is simply a question of the mathematics of the universe. Maybe all calls, or at least the good ones, come from deep inside, a deep intuition, a place of knowing that sits in our bones and in our *kishkes*. As they say in the old urban legend, "The call is coming from inside the house." That would be okay too. Being locally sourced doesn't prevent us from holding it with the honor that we would if it were undeniably divine. Maybe in holding it that way, it becomes divine.

There is one epilogue to this strange story. Another dream about my mother, but I didn't dream this one. It was dreamt by an acquaintance and Kinsey Sicks fan who called me urgently one day because my mother had come to him in a dream, asking him to convey a message. I listened to the message, which didn't feel all that urgent to me, and felt the Litvak in me putting up a wall. *Really?* I thought. *I should believe this why?* Not to mention my injured vanity: the *nerve* of someone else to dream about my mother. In good lawyerly fashion, I asked him why he thought my mother would've come to him with a message when she could've come to me directly. He said, "Funny, I asked her that. She said that you were so busy, she didn't want to bother you."

Words my mother had, of course, said to me a million times. Maybe it's coincidence. Or maybe, like in the Chasidic stories, the skeptical Litvak – the doubter in me – gets won over.

Oath of Disloyalty

On August 19, 2019, President Trump stated that Jews who vote for Democrats are guilty of either ignorance or "gross disloyalty." This poem was my response.

August 21, 2019

I am a disloyal Jew.
I am not loyal to a political party,
nor will I be loyal to dictators and mad kings.
I am not loyal to walls or cages.
I am not loyal to taunts or tweets.
I am not loyal to hatred, to Jew-baiting,
to the gloating connivings of white supremacy.

I am a disloyal Jew.
I am not loyal to any foreign power,
nor to abuse of power at home.
I am not loyal to a legacy of conquest, erasure and exploitation.
I am not loyal to stories that tell me who I should hate.

I am a loyal Jew.
I am loyal to the inconveniences of kindness.
I am loyal to the dream of justice.

I am loyal to this suffering Earth
and to all life.
I am not loyal to any founding fathers,
but I am loyal to the children who will come
and to the quality of world we leave them.

I am not loyal to what America has become,
but I am loyal to what America could be.
I am loyal to Emma Lazarus,
to huddled masses,
to freedom and welcome,
holiness, hope, and love.

The Parable of the Toyota in the Gully

It was three months into the new war, the terrible war, and I was back in Israel. When people heard I was going, they would ask in a reverential tone about my plans. They presumed that an American rabbi going to Israel in this moment of violence and heartbreak must be on a mission – witnessing the destruction or picking fruit in the abandoned kibbutzim of the south. But my assignment in Israel was and is always more modest. My 88- and 93-year-old in-laws live in Haifa, and I go to offer companionship and support. I schedule doctors' appointments, do grocery runs, change light bulbs, get them out of the house when possible.

Haifa, sitting on Mt. Carmel in Israel's north, is beyond the reach of Gazan missiles, and Lebanon seemed contented with closer targets. So Haifa was a place where a stranger could fool themselves into believing that no war was happening at all, but the illusion would be temporary. The war was everywhere. You could overhear it in the quiet, insistent conversations in cafes. You could feel it in the stiffly cordial interactions between Jews and Arabs in this famously integrated city. One turn of the head would bring into view wheat-pasted posters with the faces of hostages, official placards promoting unity and victory, and scrawled graffiti condemning the Prime Minister and demanding new elections. In this small country, even in Haifa, everyone knows someone who knows someone who was a victim of the October 7th Hamas attack. Everyone has one degree of separation from one of the hostages, so the wounds of October

7th remain unprocessed, buzzing just under the surface.

There were other strange reminders of the war. For instance, to deflect missile attacks, the Israeli military had scrambled the GPS coordinates of major cities. So if I tried to use GoogleMaps to get directions to a relative's home, it might tell me I was not in Haifa at all but in Beirut, and I was left to wander aimlessly, literally disoriented.

While in Israel I noticed that news coverage of the war in Gaza was primarily reportage of a military operation. There was a noticeable lack of public discussion and media about the suffering in Gaza, as if the shocked Israeli psyche couldn't reach that far. Coming from the outside, I felt that suffering in my body. It was a record cold and rainy clip in the country, and I spent numerous sleepless nights in my in-laws' tenth floor apartment, with wind howling, shutters clattering, and cries of jackals from the wadi below. I presumed the storm must also be in Gaza, less than two hours away, and I wondered if any of the displaced children were warm and dry. I tossed and turned and tears came.

I didn't go to Israel with a mission, but I sat with a friend, someone dear to me, who had spent October 7 barricaded with friends in a safe room on a southern kibbutz, as machine gun fire and grenades rang out all around. He told me about trying to keep his friends' children occupied and calm in that dark and stifling room until they were ultimately rescued. He told me about the days since, back home in sleepy Haifa, where the trauma is more national than individual, rendering his direct wounds of that terrible day invisible to the people around him. I put on my best pastoral manner, meeting his pain with gentle sympathy. Then it would all flood back to me, echoing through my tearful and sleepless nights.

While in Israel, I did manage to attend a national meeting of Standing Together, an organization of Jews and Palestinians coming together to dream a shared future, since there will be a future of some sort, and someone has to offer a vision of what it could be. I was moved by the words and I felt sadness at how little of the Israeli left is left. Who is there to oppose the growing extremism that fuels this war?

Even without a mission, I did have one official task to accomplish: to go to Jerusalem and pick up a handwritten megillah that our synagogue had purchased from a scribe. Friends said, "Don't drive; take the train," but I had reached a point of sadness and agitation where I just wanted to be away from other humans. A few hours of intercity driving would be my refuge, or so I thought when I climbed into my in-laws' long-parked Toyota. A half hour out of Haifa, the traffic slowed to a stop. Did it have to do with the GPS scrambling? I don't know, but by the time I reached the town of Netanya, I pulled off. I always prefer creeping along on surface streets to sitting still on a freeway. Meanwhile, Rinat, a friend and congregant who was in Israel caring for her ill father, texted me, offering to accompany me to Jerusalem. I perked up at this offer; going alone was an errand, but with Rinat it would be a true mission. We would be a delegation on behalf of the Jews of Cotati, California. She sent me her father's address in Herzliya, and I plunked it into GoogleMaps.

The app predicted it would take an hour and a half to get to Herzliya, which normally should have been only 20 minutes away. I rolled along surface streets, following the GPS's calm and confident voice. She instructed me to turn onto streets that turned out to be blocked to automobile traffic, and then she would have to recalculate when I had no choice but to decline. I could see in the distance that the freeway traffic was now moving, yet she didn't direct me onto the freeway. She sent me on back roads, and then through a construction site where I had to negotiate my way around cement mixers. Then onto a gravel road which became a dirt road, which became a gully under a bridge leading into a deeply trenched and broken tractor path through a vineyard. Finally, I was driving on something that didn't resemble a road in any way. But the transition from urban streets to this had been gradual, and despite my doubt I wanted to believe. I was curious where this was going to lead. Maybe the disaster ahead was too attractive to resist.

Rocks began banging on the bottom of the Toyota, and finally I stopped, 20 minutes or so later than any of you clearer-thinking folk would have. I stopped because I knew I would eventually – no, imminently! – wreck the car, and then I'd have to explain to some tow truck driver and to my in-laws why I had believed the GPS when she told me to go on paths that were obviously not in my self-interest. It was the anticipation of shame that finally stopped me.

I oh-so-carefully backed down the vineyard and the gully. I backed all the way to the bridge, pausing under it to get out of the car and breathe and break the spell that the GPS had somehow cast over me. I was trembling, and if I'd had a cigarette on me, I'd have taken up smoking in that moment. I got back in and tried to map a way out, but again GoogleMaps was sending me places where cars couldn't go. I turned off the app. I then drove and drove in an uncertain direction on an unknown highway until I saw the welcome offer of coffee and a table. I sat there and sipped my cappuccino, trying to breathe through tears of frustration and all the underlying layers of sorrow, where those tears were ultimately sourced.

Eventually, I picked up the phone to look at the GPS app and see if I could diagnose the problem. Sure enough, when I had entered Rinat's father's address, my clumsy thumb had grazed the bicycle icon. GoogleMaps thought I was out for a day of mountain biking and was keeping me as far from speeding cars and highways as possible.

I was too exhausted to laugh. The grief and exhaustion in my body wouldn't let go of the experience. Instead, they demanded that this turn of events not be relegated to the anecdote heap but instead be read immediately as parable. And indeed, there was a very live question in me: how it is that we can listen to a voice in our ear, directing us on paths that we know will lead to disaster, and still not question it?

This is the moment we inhabit, for Israelis certainly and for Jews in general. For years we have had a voice of rightwing nationalism whispering in our ear, passing itself off as a voice of benign Jewish fulfillment. It has been whispering to us, guiding us on paths that are ever more treacherous, more damaging, and more difficult to pull back from. We have abandoned our compass and yielded to the reassurances of a voice that experience should tell us not to trust. The Parable of the Toyota in the Gully reminds us that we each have a moral compass and we cannot afford to abandon it.

I finished my coffee and was at Rinat's in 20 minutes, chik-chak. Together, we arrived on a tree-lined corner of hilly Jerusalem and took into our hands the brand-new scroll of warm deerskin and bright ink, marveling at it and then stowing it in a Glenfiddich canister for safe travel. We ate lunch in the Arab town of Abu Ghosh, where Rinat repeatedly drew Palestinian storekeepers into conversation about the situation, in the insistently compassionate way that is her signature. Back in Haifa, I had five more domestic days with my in-laws – cooking, home reparis, and writing out helpful to-do lists that I'm sure were dispatched to the recycling bin immediately upon my departure.

At last I was on the train from Haifa to the airport, bound for home. The hills and fields were bright green from the unusual rains. It's easy to see the biblical in this landscape – hills traversed by kings and prophets and apostles of Jesus. It's easy to picture centuries of Ottoman rule, a land filled with Arab farmers and their Jewish neighbors. This is a land formed by romantic ideas and terrible destructions, not unlike our own country, and there is no going back. The road only extends forward.

I leaned back in my train seat, wrung out, and tried to imagine a future gentler than the present. As the train rocked me to sleep, I offered my tattered prayers for all who are suffering, trapped, angry, hungry. How many tears have watered this land? When will all its inhabitants reap in joy?

The Bittersweet Exchange

It's a wrap! The papers are signed. The inspections inspected. The repairs repaired. The movers have loaded 42 boxes, 2 suitcases and 3 pieces of furniture onto a truck in the driveway, drawing to a close the life of the Keller family on Osceola Avenue in Niles, Illinois. Three years prior, the house was full of life: 55 years of life lived, plus another half century of accumulated history piled high in boxes in the basement.

In the two and half years since our mother died, my sister Lynn and I have come back repeatedly to make headway on closing out that history. To sort, curate, designate, and haul. And the house – not the frame but the content, not the body but the soul – has effected a kind of *tzimtzum*. A contraction. Each time we are there, the house recedes some, as if wondering about its own existence and finding it no longer necessary. With this trip, with these last things removed, *poof!* What was the Keller house has disappeared altogether.

Over this time, every piece of furniture was considered, offered, allotted, and carried out the door. Every piece of paper was reviewed, read, released, or retained for one or more rounds of future consideration. Every photo was appreciated. The life of every forebear – parents, grandparents, great-grandparents, great aunts and uncles – was examined, discussed, and liberated from a dull shell of forgetfulness, like an egg broken into a bowl on a hungry winter morning. The physical objects of my mother's life have been dealt out like cards to many players: friends, cousins, charities, theaters, libraries, untold numbers of strangers, many of whom came to the house and, in bittersweet exchange, shared their stories and told how the bed/computer/chair/coat rack would change something for them.

The work was not steady or linear. We'd do five-day spurts — maybe an aggregate of six weeks of heavy labor over two years. We would swim upstream through symbolism and memory. We'd get momentum and we'd get sidetracked. There were a million instant research projects, trying to crack the mysteries of unidentifiable things: people in photos, sources of memorabilia, the meaning of markings on silver platters.

Our final research project had an inconclusive outcome. It was to determine the provenance of a quilted bedspread folded and wrapped in plastic. It had been folded and wrapped in that same plastic for as long as Lynn and I could remember. Neither of us knew whose it was or how it came into the house, and there's no one left to ask. But there was a dry-cleaning tag on it. "North Chicago Laundry." And there was a phone number on the tag: Bi8-3210. No one has advertised phone numbers with letter prefixes since the end of the 1960s, so it had seemingly been there, clean and wrapped, for at least that long.

The dry-cleaning ticket was a clue. If we could work out where this laundry was, it might tell us who this bedspread belonged to, since no city dweller walks more than two blocks for a dry cleaner. With Google's help, we searched the name of the laundry. Too generic. Then we tried to determine which neighborhood had been the Bi8 telephone exchange. Because sometimes the exchange itself was the neighborhood's name, like "Diversey" or "Hyde Park."

Lynn and I both remember the days of letter prefixes in phone numbers. Our own telephone number, as we first learned it as children, began with YO, for Yorktown, although there has never been a nearby anything called Yorktown. Skokie was OR, for Orchard, and we allowed that there might once have been orchards where now Jews grew like so much fruit. And the exchanges in the city? I had no idea what they stood for; they just helped me remember phone numbers. Aunt Hattie was EA7; Aunt Birdie GR6.

As this tangent ruptured our planned work, or at least mine (Lynn had moved on to puzzling over fragile 78-rpm records and an old Spirograph set), I learned that Illinois Bell in the 1920s had adopted a calling system for Chicago involving 3-letter exchanges followed by four numerals. This limited each exchange to 9,999 phones, for instance EAS 0001 through EAS 9999. But the City was growing! In 1948, Illinois Bell increased the available phone numbers tenfold by switching to a system of 2 letters and 5 numerals. The existing exchanges were slimmed down to two letters followed by a number. Now each exchange could have 99,999 phones!

At the beginning, the digit following the two opening letters was the numeric equivalent of the letter that had been there in the exchange's name all along. The EAS of "Eastgate" became EA7. GR6 was a restatement of the old GRO, for "Grovehill." Complete 7-digit numeric dialing only became available on September 11, 1960. My parents wouldn't notice, being busy in the hospital, welcoming their new son.

And Bi8, the exchange for our mystery laundry? It was the new articulation of BIT, short for "Bittersweet." It seemed unrelated to any actual place. Perhaps it was just plucked from the official AT&T list of recommended exchange names. Either way, we were now chasing a bedspread back to a dry cleaner at Bittersweet 8-3210.

At last we found the goods. The Bittersweet exchange was Near North – Lincoln Park-ish – and we then discovered the laundry at 2901 N. Clybourn. Who in the family lived near there? I can't imagine. Not a neighborhood I remember visiting as a child. I could return to this mystery one day, liberating Mom's and Grandma Sade's old address books from the storage boxes they now inhabited.

Most likely, I'll never know, and that's a new sensation, one I'll have to get used to.

All the grounding objects and personalities of Osceola Avenue are now free-floating. Contents of boxes have gotten mixed or combined in packing, and in doing so, we've deprived ourselves of future clues. From this point forward, it will be hard to say, "This came from Aunt Hattie's." On the other hand, it will be easy and true and all that's necessary to say, "This came from Marilyn's."

The famous basement is empty. The bedrooms, the kitchen too. The patio is bare, the grass overgrown. It's done. This home is gone. With a last sigh, it has withdrawn from that physical structure and from the world. Going forward, it can only be carried in our memories. This isn't news. It's just that today is the day beyond which no other illusion can be maintained.

As I walk out the door for the last time, I instinctively place my hand on the doorpost, in the spot where the *mezuzah* had, until today, hung. I know it is our custom to touch the *mezuzah* to invoke the Divine in our comings and goings. But in this moment, I realize we also do it to invoke home itself.

All things change. People come and go. Losses are inevitable; we all experience them. The *new* edges in and considers the vacant space. Light gives way to dark and back to light. Life breathes us in and breathes us out again. An easy, bittersweet exchange – sad, rich, beautiful, inescapable.

Taking Sides

October 17, 2023

Today I am taking sides.

I am taking the side of Peace.
Peace, which I will not abandon
even when its voice is drowned out
by hurt and hatred,
bitterness of loss,
cries of right and wrong.

I am taking the side of Peace
whose name has barely been spoken
in this winnerless war.

I will hold Peace in my arms,
and share my body's breath,
lest Peace be added
to the body count.

I will call for de-escalation
even when I want nothing more
than to get even.
I will do it
in the service of Peace.

I will make a clearing
in the overgrown
thicket of cause and effect
so Peace can breathe
for a minute
and reach for the sky.

I will do what I must
to save the life of Peace.
I will breathe through tears.
I will swallow pride.
I will bite my tongue.
I will offer love
without testing for deservingness.

So don't ask me to wave a flag today
unless it is the flag of Peace.
Don't ask me to sing an anthem
unless it is a song of Peace.
Don't ask me to take sides
unless it is the side of Peace.

Glossary of Hebrew and Yiddish Terms

Bashert – predestined; meant to be.

Bat Kol – a Divine voice.

Bimah – the raised pulpit of a synagogue.

Challah – a braided Sabbath bread.

Chayot – celestial beings with four faces – human, ox, lion, and eagle, according to Ezekiel's vision.

Chazan – the cantor or prayer leader.

Chelm – a town in eastern Poland whose Jewish residents were notoriously illogical, at least according to a popular storytelling tradition.

Cherubim – celestial beings whose winged image was forged in gold for the *mishkan*.

Chesed – the divine quality of generosity and kindness.

Chik-chak – in no time at all.

Chutzpah – nerve, audacity.

Chasidic – pertaining to the movement begun by Rabbi Israel Ba'al Shem Tov in 18th-Century Ukraine. Chasidism is characterized by ecstatic song, prayer, and dance; by the study of mystical texts; and by privileging the spirit's intention as equal in importance to scholarship. Chasidic courts grew around charismatic, often wonder-working rabbis called *rebbes*.

Gematria – a practice of finding meaning in sacred text by assigning numeric values to letters and deriving mathematical correspondences among words.

Gevurah – the divine quality of strength and structure.

Go'el – one who redeems from danger or bondage.

Haftarah – the weekly reading of a preset selection from one of the books of the Prophets.

Kabbalah / kabbalist / kabbalistic – referring to any of Judaism's mystical traditions.

Kabbalat Shabbat – the prayer service marking the arrival of the Sabbath.

Kaddish – an Aramaic prayer of praise, notably recited by mourners in honor of the dead.

Kadesh / K'deshah – a priest/ess of a goddess in Israelite antiquity, often disparagingly translated as "ritual prostitute."

Kapoteh – a long wool or gabardine coat worn by Chasidic men.

Kiddush – the blessing over the wine and, in its long form, honoring the arrival of Shabbat.

Kishkes – the intestines, the gut (both literally and metaphorically).

Kodesh Kodashim – the Holy of Holies, the innermost chamber of the *mishkan* or of the ancient Temple in Jerusalem.

Lecha Dodi – a late medieval hymn by Shlomo Halevi Alkabetz to welcome the Sabbath.

Lulav – a wand of combined palm, myrtle, and willow branches waved on the holiday of Sukkot.

Ma'ariv Aravim – the evening prayer, praising God as the designer of light and dark, day and night.

Mah'pach, Pashta, Katon – three of the musical figures used to chant words of Torah.

Malach (pl. *Malachim*) – an angel or messenger.

Malchut – the quality of divine immanence (literally "kingdom" or "realm").

Mechayeh – something refreshing or enlivening.

Megillah – a hand-scribed scroll of the Book of Esther

Mezuzah (pl. *mezuzot*) – a small box affixed to the doorpost containing a parchment with the words of the Shema.

Mikveh – a ritual bath.

Mishkan – the holy tent in which the ark of the covenant was kept during the wandering of the Israelites in the desert.

Mitzrayim – Hebrew for "Egypt"

Neshamah or neshomeh – the soul.

Niggun or *nign* (pl. *niggunim*) – a wordless melody, deriving from the Chasidic tradition.

Ofanim – celestial beings of some round shape, described as the wheels of the chariot in Ezekiel's vision.

Omer – the 49 days between Passover and Shavuot; a week of weeks.

Oneg Shabbat – refreshments to delight the palate after a Sabbath prayer service.

Rokeach – perfumer or chemist.

Sefirah – any one of ten divine qualities or energies that form the machinery of Creation.

Seraphim – fiery angels with six wings, as seen in the vision of Isaiah.

Shabbos / Shabbat – the seventh day or Sabbath; a day of rest and devotion.

Shechinah – the immanent presence of the Divine, also the Divine Feminine.

Shema – a central Jewish prayer declaring God's oneness, beginning with the word Shema, "listen!"

Shir HaShirim – the biblical book Song of Songs.

Shtetl (pl. *shtetlech*) – a predominantly Jewish village of Eastern Europe.

Shtibl – a small synagogue or prayer-house.

Shtreiml (pl. *shtreimlech*) – a large fur hat worn by some Chasidic men.

Shul – a synagogue.

Tallit – a prayer shawl.

Tiferet – the divine quality of truth, beauty, and balance. Tiferet is seen as the synthesis of the qualities of *chesed* and *gevurah*.

Tish – literally a table; a gathering around a table presided over by a Chasidic *rebbe*.

Treyf – unkosher.

Yeshivah – a Talmudic academy.

Yeshivah Bocher – a student in a yeshivah.

Yeshivah shel Ma'lah – the heavenly court in which legal rulings are issued from on high.

Yontiff – a Jewish holy day

Acknowledgments

I have had loving family around me throughout my life, and I know from my work, alas, what a rarity that can be. I am held in the close embrace of family of origin and family forged: Anne and Suegee Tamar-Mattis, our next generation Squid and Ari, my sister and friend Lynn Keller and her partner Susan Draus, my brothers-in-law and neighbors Elon Slozberg and Doron Hovav, my parents-in-law, Rheta and Mitch Slozberg. Grandparents, great aunts, and great-grandmothers enlivened my childhood and continue to inhabit my imagination and my dreams. The ancestors stand at my back.

A battery of people supported my rabbinate and pushed me hard to share my writing more widely. These include Shari Brenner, Shoshana Fershtman, Anna Belle Kaufman, Emily Doskow, and, with special determination, Dr. Rachel Naomi Remen. I was encouraged in my creativity and my seriousness, against their own interest, by the members of the Kinsey Sicks, America's Favorite Dragapella Beautyshop Quartet, most especially the last configuration that I was part of: Jeff Manabat, Spencer Brown, and my soul-sister, Ben Schatz.

I have had more beloved teachers than I could name, including Rabbi Shohama Harris Wiener, Rabbi Marcia Prager, Rabbi Leila Gal-Berner, and my friend and mentor, Rabbi Elliot Ginsburg. I have been enriched by langourous time with brilliant study partners and colleagues: Rabbi Eli Herb, Rabbi Amy Grossblatt Pessah,

Rabbi Eli Cohen, and Rabbi Diane Elliot. I hold with abiding love the memory of two teachers who, I think and hope, live in me: Rabbi Mark S. Shapiro and Rabbi Danny Leifer.

I am grateful beyond measure to the people of Congregation Ner Shalom – a plucky, creative, brilliant, colorful, holy community that arrived at just the right moment of my life, after all my dreams of being a rabbi had been surrendered; and to the Taproot Community, who continue to challenge and inspire me, giving me hope for the future, and offering me a place to try out being an elder.

The beginnings of this book came through a pivotal writing retreat at the Mesa Refuge in Pt. Reyes Station, CA. I am grateful to Susan Page Tillett for inviting me and to Commonweal in Bolinas for nominating me. Drafts of this book were reviewed with great care and insight by Orren Perlman, Anna Belle Kaufman, and Emily Doskow. Diane Frank at Blue Light Press has been an encouraging, kind, and perceptive editor and mentor at every step.

Ultimately, what makes this life sweetest is my husband of 16 or 20 or 30 years, depending how you count, Oren Slozberg. *Where you go, I will go.*

About the Author

Irwin Keller is the spiritual leader of Congregation Ner Shalom in Sonoma County, California and a co-founder of the Taproot Community. He was the primary author of Chicago's first gay rights law, in force since 1989. He was a co-founder and, for 21 years, a performer with the Kinsey Sicks, America's Favorite Dragapella Beautyshop Quartet. He is ordained through the ALEPH Alliance for Jewish Renewal, in the lineage of Rabbi Zalman Schachter-Shalomi. He lives on Sonoma Mountain with his husband, their co-parents, and two empty rooms from which the children launched. His blog, *Itzik's Well*, can be found at irwinkeller.com.

Printed in the USA
CPSIA information can be obtained
at www.ICGtesting.com
LVHW091623240824
789029LV00001B/1